DO NOT REMOVE
CARDS FROM POCKET

Sin in the Secular Age

Sin in the Secular Age

Bernard Häring, C.Ss.R.

Doubleday & Company, Inc.
Garden City, New York
1974

ISBN: 0-385-09017-X
Library of Congress Catalog Card Number 73–10539
Copyright © 1974 by Bernard Häring
All Rights Reserved
Printed in the United States of America

Acknowledgments

In spite of my interest in the matter, this book would probably never have been written without the persistent and convincing invitation of Mr. John Delaney, my editor at Doubleday, to write it. I want to thank him for his interest and encouragement. I am also grateful to my students of the Academia Alfonsiana who worked with me on seminars on this subject.

As in the preparation of a number of my previous books I could always call on the most generous help of Sr. Gabrielle L. Jean, Ph.D. She did most of the typewriting besides taking care of correct English. Mrs. Josephine Ryan helped me on parts of the manuscript with the same generosity.

Contents

Introduction

The new worldview, the new mode of experience of life, the greater breadth of dialog in an era of mass media and the jet, the critical spirit of our age, and many other things challenge today's ethicist and theologian to reflect more boldly on the meaning, concept, and sense of sin. I am trying to do this in a theological and pastoral perspective in such a way that all our talk about sin will be understood in the context of redemption and liberation, as a call to conversion and to a commitment to renewal and reform.

I shall try to remain mindful of the fact that the heart of moral theology, and particularly in a treatise on sin, is the gospel. Only in the light of the gospel, and of law and order insofar as they are part of the gospel, can we speak meaningfully on sin and liberation from sin. Thus a treatise on sin is essentially a way of speaking of redemption and salvation; we cannot speak of sin in itself (*in se*). Our interest is not so much in sin as in sinful mankind and the person in the context of salvation history: man coming ever more to the realization that he is in further need of purification when he accepts the calling to ongoing conversion and liberation.

As a prelude to our treatise on sin, let us consider the various levels of the concept of sin.

1. THE PREMORAL AND INFRAMORAL LEVEL

People sometimes speak of "sin" when nothing more or little more than social pressure is involved: "You should not do this" or "if you do this you must accept the sanctions," which usually means some damage to one's social role. The important element is the social sanction and discrimination. In other words, people may speak of sin and the penalties of sin when what is at stake is only conformance or nonconformance to social pressures or prejudices.

Whatever is taboo in a certain social context belongs to the pre- and inframoral level, yet people—even intelligent people—seldom dare to challenge certain of these prohibitions. They simply accept them because nobody dares or nobody is allowed to question them.

However, we should not forget that often in a taboo attitude and in social pressures there can be a strange admixture of enslavement and a dawning moral consciousness.

2. THE MORAL LEVEL

Sin is equated here with moral disorder. This is an approach to morality on the humanistic or the horizontal level. It pertains to man's own self-perfection and respect for the common good. On this level, the whole vision can be static or dynamic.

On the static level, moral disorder or moral "sin" is in any action that can disturb the established order. Even the courage to take risks, to expose oneself to danger is considered sinful. In an uncritical conviction that the established authority, tradition, and law are unquestionally good, any disobedience to these moral powers is considered a disorder or morally bad.[1]

1. This description accords rather well with the "conventional moral" stage noted in Professor Kenneth Keniston's article on moral development (*The Critic*, September–October, 1969, pp. 17–24), where he also discussed Lawrence Kohlberg's studies on the various stages of moral thinking and development.

A dynamic worldview equates moral defection with failure to do the good that one could do, in order to develop one's own insight, one's own sensitivity, freedom, and creativity. Sin is a failure or refusal to grow or to work for one's own social integration. Moral disorder is a refusal of responsibility and coresponsibility, and implies all forms of behavior that diminish a man's ability or capacity to become a fitting member of the community.

3. THE RELIGIOUS LEVEL

On the religious level, where a man is confronted with the sphere of the sacred, we can properly speak of sin. As long as we stay only on the moral level, we should do better to restrict our terminology to expressions such as "moral disorder" or "moral failure." An example may help to explain the difficulty of speaking of sin in a secularized age, particularly where there is not only secularization but real secularism.

During my stay in Russia, I talked with a group of women who told me quite candidly about the number of abortions they had undergone during the time the Communist Party was promoting abortion. At one point I was truly horrified by these records and asked unthinkingly, "Did you not consider this sinful?" The reaction clearly indicated that this question made no sense to them. I therefore asked, "What did you think of the moral value of your behavior?" The question was then intelligible, and the response was, "Of course we realized somehow that all this was harmful to us; it was degrading and sometimes even shameful."

With Rudolf Otto, theologians distinguish sins directly opposed to the sphere of the sacred or sins against the sacred ethos, from sins against the sanctioned ethos, against the moral values, traditions, and precepts that supposedly have been sanctioned by the religious sphere. This distinction corresponds to the traditional distinctions between sins against the theological virtues of faith, hope, and love of God, against

God's right to be worshiped, and on the other hand, sins against those moral values and virtues that were always understood to be sanctioned through faith.

Because modern man's thinking has been deeply affected by secularization and at least partially by secularism and horizontalism, he has considerable difficulty in understanding or rightly appreciating the meaning of sins against the sacred ethos. To some extent this difficulty is due also to reaction against an exaggerated catalogue of sins that directly opposed the sacred ethos as it was understood by a certain priestly tradition.

An earlier sacralizing era made so many things "sacred" that sin was often not understood as sin against the holy God but rather as sin against the too sacralized, too sacred things that had no clear relation to God's call to love and trust. In a certain priestly tradition there was such overemphasis on sacred prescriptions, sacred traditions, sacred rituals, vestments, and so on, which were uncritically sanctioned "by God's authority," that today's critical man can ask whether or not that tradition really knew much about the holy God who is not at the disposal of man's arbitrary decisions.

Desacralization in an era of secularization is a holy duty for all those who believe in God, who alone is holy, and want to make the gospel present in its full credibility to today's critical world. Hence, at this moment in history, we have to return to the great prophetic tradition that reached its summit in Christ. There, sin is seen above all as a lack of knowledge of God or a falsified image of God, and is manifested by lack of love and mercy. It is the unjust and merciless attitude toward our neighbor and especially toward the poor. It is refusal of the Covenant.

The direction of our effort in this book is pointed by the biblical statement, "The Sabbath was made for man and not man for the Sabbath" (Mk. 2:27). In the first part, "the Sabbath was made for man," is found the religious dimension or expression of faith. Man truly needs periods of time reserved for adoration; he needs the common worship of the one God in order not to become an idol worshiper or the slave of worldly structures. The second part, "man was not made for the Sabbath," protests against a wrong sacralization of the Sabbath. As we probe into the deeper meaning of this statement, we shall uncover the true sense of sin against the honor due to God and against the dignity and development of man.

1

Change of Focus

The following pages will try to trace the changes in emphases and perspectives in moral theology that have resulted to a great extent from the processes of secularization and desacralization.

1. FROM A MORAL THEOLOGY FOR CONFESSORS AND PENITENTS TO A MORAL THEOLOGY OF LIFE

Ethical prophetism is a true call to confess one's sins before God and before the people; but much more than that, it is a call to be converted to the living God and to the real issues of life.

Through Christ the Prophet, the whole moral message is one of an everlasting life, which begins in a decisive way here on earth. From this stems a morality of the Paschal Mystery, of the Eucharistic man, the man who becomes aware of the new life in Christ, who died for all so that men should never again live only for themselves but rather with Christ and for their fellow men. It is a morality of gratitude and service, the morality signified by the Eucharistic celebration.

Sin, then, is everything that opposes the message and the joy of the Paschal Mystery. It is lack of gratitude for redemption, and a deliberate refusal to put to death one's selfish self. This has always been the chief orientation of the best Christian morality and spiritual theology.

Through a quite different approach in the mode of administration of the sacrament of penance, initiated in the Irish Church and legalized in a modified form by the Fourth Lateran Council in 1215, a certain change in emphasis gradually occurred. However, not until after the Council of Trent did the main effort of moral theology turn decisively toward training confessors. Its perspective gave a one-sided emphasis to the priest's role as judge and controller, and as a result, moral theology became obsessed with juridical problems: "What is a mortal sin that must be confessed before going to communion? What can the priest absolve? What kind of solutions can he give?"

The new perspective of today's moral theology was already expressed about 150 years ago by Bishop John Michael Sailer of Ratisbon, who gave his work the significant title, "Moral Theology for Lay People as Well as for Priests." In full awareness of the consequences of such a change in focus, in view of the addresses, I gave to my own treatise *The Law of Christ* some twenty years ago the subtitle, "Moral Theology for Lay People and for Priests." This approach eliminated all the questions primarily concerned with the priest as judge or confessor in the confessional, but it had even greater consequences in the total perspective. Only recently has the whole community of moral theologians, and gradually also the magisterium of the Church, become fully conscious of all the values in this new focus.

2. FROM A STATIC TO A MORE DYNAMIC VISION OF LIFE AND SIN

Jesus condemns with particular severity the sins of the Pharisees: their self-sufficiency, their self-complacency, and their static view of law and tradition. He accuses them,

"How well you have succeeded in making God's own command null and void in favor of your own traditions" (Mt. 15:6). They had lost contact with life, which is growth and development, an ever-new challenge, and had become so stubborn, so rigid that they could withstand the Holy Spirit even when confronted with the unique revelation of God in Jesus Christ.

Jesus' own moral message is simple and direct: "Be converted and put your trust in the Gospel" (Mk. 1:14). Under the dynamic force of the Gospel we are called to an ongoing conversion and to watchfulness for the presence of God in the ever-new opportunities to serve our brothers.

Medieval thought concentrated on the moral exigencies around the concept of order (*ordo*). As originally expressed by St. Augustine, this was a beautiful idea: the order of love (*ordo amoris*) demanding constant growth toward an unselfish dialectic and thence to an ever-greater breakthrough to Christlike love. However, under the influence of the political and social order, the whole thinking about the moral order and transgressions against it became increasingly fixed in a static mold. This political trend climaxed in the Congress of Vienna (1816) in the "sacred alliance" between the conservative powers: Czar of Russia, Emperor of Prussia, Emperor of Austria, the Bourbons in France and Spain, with the Pope as supreme emperor of the states of the Church. The awakening that has led to a new theology of revolution and liberation can easily be understood as a profound nonviolent revolution of the Gospel.

The cultural awareness of today's elite is characterized by a certain "futurology," a realization that today's generations are responsible for the generations to come. There is a dynamic concept of man's nature in the perspective of human history. Added to this is the prominent role of the psychology of development and maturation, and of the sociology that studies the growth and decay of cultures. In such a climate, a static approach to life is a serious sin and the beginning of unavoidable decay.

3. Sin Against Man's Nature in the Perspective of Historicity

Our dynamic age, with its perception of the evolution and development of past ages, has revolutionized the concept of sin against man's nature. Under the impact of the Restoration and of rationalism, the static view of natural law saw all efforts of courageous solutions to new problems as sins against human nature. We now see more clearly the time-bound character of so many formulations of natural law and the impact of erroneous and sinful social structures and attitudes on the very formulations of natural law and sins against natural law.

Today's worldview reveals the sinfulness of clinging to past formulations that do not correspond to the available knowledge, shared experience, and coreflections of this newer age. Man is a responsible steward of his whole heritage, cultural and biological. Because of this, sins of omission can be quite as grave as sins of commission in this matter.

4. A Shift from a Predominantly Priestly, Clerical Vision of Sin toward a Prophetic Desacralization

The impact of secularization on the priestly concept of sin has been cataclysmic. If, however, believers remain vigilant and accept the challenge, secularization may be seen in the future as one of the most beneficial events in the history of salvation. Faced with the consciousness of a secular age, biblical renewal has discovered Christ, the Prophet, with unprecedented intuition and sagacity.

Most of the world religions and Christian churches have withstood the prophetic wrath of Karl Marx, who accused religion of alienation and of an alienating sacralization. It was right and necessary that the Church should condemn his conclusions, which denied the existence of God and of man's need for religion; but only at the Second Vatican Council did the official Church recognize, fully and humbly, that wrong religious doctrines and a life alienated from the Gospel are among the main causes of atheism. "Taken as a whole, atheism is not a spontaneous development but stems from a variety of causes, including a critical reaction against religious beliefs and, in some places, against the Christian religion in particular. Hence believers can have more than a little to do with the birth of atheism" (*GS* 19).

Since atheism and secularism are the most serious threats to man's freedom and happiness, the whole of theology, and particularly moral theology and a treatise on sin, must be fully aware of their accusations and challenges.

With so many laws, precepts, and threats of mortal sin that have little or nothing to do with human dignity and the "adoration of God in spirit and truth," we can understand the reaction of secularists who consider religion irrelevant. We have to accept the challenge, knowing that whatever makes religion and the teaching about sin irrelevant to life is itself a great sin against the Church's universal mission to proclaim the gospel and to help all men become believers and adorers of God in spirit and in truth.

Even within the Church there is a great tendency toward reaction instead of synthesis. One of these reactions is called "horizontalism," which gives little or no attention to the transcendence of God and to adoration, and thus sins gravely against the prophetic synthesis of the Old and New Testaments. However, all efforts to define sins against the sacred in a merely verticalist and therefore separatist attitude are also responsible for the tensions and lack of synthesis. We have to realize that a wrathful youth and a whole critical generation will never accept any concept of sin that hinders personal commitment to peace and justice on earth or that does not at least awaken personal energies in this directon. The situation demands a new balance between the sacred and the sanctioned ethos, and a new definition of both, in view of the living God and of the real problems of life.

In the context of secularization and a charismatic prophetic renewal, we have to give a new response to the problem that is already treated prophetically in Matthew (Ch. 25) and in Romans (Ch. 2), whereby those who have transcended their own self-interest in generous dedication to their neighbor and to the common good can be saved, although they have not come to explicit faith and may even have rejected the faith of those who felt rich and secure in their formulations. The question has to be asked the other way around: "*Quis dives salvetur?*" Can the "rich man," who is not concerned with the yearning of his unbeliever brother, be saved if he enshrines the message of faith in his traditionalism and his own security complex? "God has no favorites" (Rom. 2:11).

5. The Impact of the Authority Crisis on the Concept of Sin

When authority was uncritically absolutized and sacralized, schools or moralists, confessors, and the Supreme Congregation of the Holy Inquisition (the Holy Office) knew precisely what constituted mortal and what constituted venial sin. Church authorities not only dared to determine by "natural law" what was or was not mortal sin, but also to decree what they wished to be imposed "under pain of mortal sin."

The critical generation dares to ask them, "Are you so sure that God takes all your orders?" or even, "Are you sure that it is not you who sin when you dare to deal out God's judgments?" In an uncritical culture, the words of the Gospel, "Whatever you bind on earth shall be bound in heaven" and "whatever you allow on earth shall be allowed in heaven" (Mt. 18:18), and similar words, were so interpreted as to make it seem that Church authorities could take the place of

God. There was no thought that, for them too, Christ could be the saving protest. The true meaning of the message is that the responsibility and coresponsibility that frees a brother from his sin is a work that has everlasting results, and that God himself is on the side of those who earnestly guide and correct their brother. However, we should not simply invoke God and his authority if we neglect our duty of fraternal correction or attempt to overpower our neighbor.

The truly religious man feels that every expression of human authority that equates itself with God is a grave sin against the truth, "You alone are holy." To speak of Church authority in such a way that those who know Church history are seriously tempted against faith is recognized as a most serious sin against faith and the holiness of God. Many things that once were considered sacred duty—sacred wars, torture, secret denunciations without risk of punishment—are recognized today not only as moral disorders and crimes of a particular culture but truly as sins against the sacred mission of the Church to make known the all-holy and merciful God.

In the past, many precepts and laws taught by the moralists under sanction of mortal sin were ignored or never understood by the great multitude of people. In the many cases where the simple people could not understand or realize these commands, the more benevolent and merciful moralists suggested that they should be left in their "invincible ignorance" until they had reached higher levels of education and of morality. Today we realize that, on the contrary, it was often the simple people who were right and the moralists who were in invincible ignorance.

All this makes us aware that it can be a very serious sin to teach or to affirm as certain what we do not know at all, at least not with certainty. In our common effort to come to greater discernment, we would do well to reread from time to time some of the manuals which, until twenty years ago, were still in use in most seminaries. It would help us to become more humble and cautious in our own assertions.

There are also other reasons for humility and caution. The insights of depth psychology and social psychology about the limits of the conscious use of freedom and the conditions of personal and moral growth have made us particularly sensitive about attempts to judge whether others have committed mortal or venial sins. While a moralist (now in a high position) asserted some twelve years ago, in a Roman clerical review, that everyone who exposes himself to depth psychology surely commits a mortal sin, we are today rather inclined to consider it a very serious sin not to profit from all these insights in order to remove obstacles to freedom and growth in our own moral responsibilities.

6. THE NEW SENSITIVITY TO THEOLOGICAL, ETHICAL, AND CULTURAL PLURALISM

Under the influence of centralism and monolithic European or Roman thinking, legitimate efforts of people of other parts of the world to live according to their own cultural norms were considered to be serious sins. Today, after an era of colonialism, we have a particular horror of the specific form of ethical-cultural colonialism that uncritically imposes its own norms on people of other cultures. These imposed norms can do great harm to a people and to a religion.

Biblical theology, through studies of the context in which God's revelation met the people of Israel, gives us deep insights into God's own pedagogy of salvation. God did not import alien cultures and ethical norms; he purified those in existence within their own culture. In the concrete context, the various apostolic writings emphasize the urgency of one value and obligation over another. Serious hermeneutics make this clear by new insights into the contextual element of a number of ethical norms of the Old and New Testaments. It is no longer easy for us to prove the absoluteness of an ethical obligation by one or other quotation from the Bible without looking first into the cultural context of the local community in which it was formulated.

Once again we have to refer to the historicity of human nature and to the historical context of any natural-law theory. I want to illustrate the problem by the controversial issue of polygamy in a great number of African and Asian tribes. Forty years ago, most of the missionaries in Africa would have glorified as heroic an African tribesman who would dismiss his second wife in order to be baptized. Today, these same missionaries confess their sins on this issue. I heard the public confession of an older missionary who had encouraged one of his catechumens, an outstanding and highly esteemed man of his tribe, to dismiss his second wife, whom he loved dearly, as well as two older women entrusted to him according to the leviratical duty when his older brother died. The catechumen was so concerned about baptism and salvation that he yielded to the request, though with great sadness. Within one year he died, probably because of his grief at seeing the unhappiness of the two older ladies who had been accepted by his younger brothers but were not at all loved or appreciated, and the tremendous suffering of the young wife whom he had sent away. This man had also lost his social prestige and honor because he had broken the sacred obligations of his own culture and his covenants.

Today even those missionaries who do not dare to consider baptising a polygamist would not think of suggesting the disruption of a stable family unit, where this would be against the good of all the persons concerned and against the good of the community.

7. THE SHIFT FROM THE MORALITY OF ACT AND DECISION-MAKING TO A MORALITY OF CONVERSION AND RENEWAL

In no way am I suggesting that the materiality of individual acts and decisions is irrelevant. It does have great relevance for the moral situation of both individual and community.

However, we realize that the manuals of the past century considered the individual act in a very abstract and impersonal way, and that the enumeration of *per se* mortal sins often led to perverse and ironic conclusions. For instance, a man fighting temptations against chastity who ten times renewed his purpose and still relapsed, would have to confess ten mortal sins, while another, who had once deliberately planned to use the next opportunity to sin, had to confess only one.

A moral theology formulated for confessors whose first role was to be "judges" has always tended to look too exclusively at the individual act and the individual decision. Good confessors have somehow transcended this attitude, but the manuals and whole background of ecclesiastical life have favored a certain concentration on discrete acts. Now depth psychology, and developmental psychology in particular, make it easier for us to understand the biblical morality that is, above all, a call to radical conversion of heart, a call to a totally new orientation. "Make good the tree and you will have good fruits" (Mt. 12:33).

We see much more clearly today how the individual act is conditioned by a person's whole earlier development and by the rectitude of falsity of one's whole orientation. In the light of this knowledge and of the biblical doctrine of conversion, we see sin, above all, in those acts and omissions that cause a diminishment of freedom, of insight, and of sensititivy.

Europe's traditional moral theology has focused strongly on men's hearts, the ethic of attitudes and virtuous decisions, but has not paid enough attention to their social responsibilities; therefore it did not realize how much the decision of the individual act was influenced not only by good or bad will, but also by the whole historical, cultural, and moral context of one's life. Today's moral theology not only judges the omissions whereby men neglect to "make good the tree" but also emphasizes the responsibility for tending the ground where the tree grows. In other words, we resent a one-sided appeal for individual conversion of heart and mind and for better fruit, without at the same time any real examination or attention to the responsibility of those institutions, structures, public opinion media, and so on, that so greatly influence men's moral freedom and sensitivities.

Several North American Protestant schools of Christian ethics have lately been focusing so strongly on "decision-making" that the individual act of decision becomes their almost exclusive concern. This is particularly true of the individualistic situation ethics of Joseph Fletcher. He is extremely alert to the situation of the individual and the individual decision, but he does not see the total context, particularly the good of the whole community.

8. A More Personalistic Concept of Sin

Although strongly emphasizing the objective norm, the best traditional Catholic moral theology has always given final consideration to the subjective sincerity of the personal decision. The subjective or personal mortal sin has always been distinguished from an objective moral disorder. However, so many principles were absolutized and sacralized that moralists did not ask courageously enough what those principles meant for the good of the person and of individual communities.

Today's outlook is thoroughly personalistic in the sense that the desacralization of "sacred" things and traditions goes hand-in-hand with the resacralization of the human person and community of persons. There is no room for sacred biological and other impersonal laws that can oppose the truly sacred rights of persons toward development. Any imposition of abstract principles, untested against the historical context as to whether they really serve the good of persons and the community, is considered a sin against man, who is made in the image and likeness of God.

9. A Shift from Prohibitive Laws to the Main Orientations

The traditional examination of conscience looked first of all to those precepts and laws that forbade certain attitudes or, even more, certain acts. Under the influence of the biblical renewal, the psychology of development, and the whole of our dynamic culture, we again come to take more seriously the main biblical orientation expressed, for instance, in the fifth chapter of Matthew, with the seven urgent "but I tell you" amendments.

All that Christ introduces with the words, "the ancestors were told" are prohibitive laws. What he proposes instead of and beyond them are indeed normative values, but they are not to be seen in a static way. They are *goal* values for the whole of our life. This can be understood only in view of the gratuitous gifts God has bestowed upon each of us, and in the perspective of choice between development toward wholeness and decay.

A static moral theology that focuses only on limitations and prohibitions would not consider it a sin for a person to neglect his special charism. A pneumatologic theology, however, and a moral perspective that corresponds to the dynamism of our age, considers it truly a sin if one hides in the ground his second, third, or fifth talent. How much poorer would the world be if St. Francis of Assisi had not fully used his special charism and had observed only the prohibitive laws! A Christian who, having received five talents, gained deep insights and attained a high degree of freedom, is now turning away from Christ, is in a much worse moral condition than the one who is coming from afar, still laboring under a sinful past but truly on the way, slowly climbing toward the evangelical orientation, "Love one another as I have loved you." Moral disorder—sin—is seen in a perspective of the "law of growth," which coincides with the "law of grace." In a time like ours, when so many traditional laws and limiting norms are being desacralized and critically reviewed, it would be a disaster to deprive Christians of the clear orientations given by the goal commandments of the gospel. The catalogues of sin given in the Scriptures should not be considered as describing isolated acts but rather as criteria for discernment of what can and cannot be done in the name of redeemed and redeeming love.

10. THE SHIFT FROM A GENERALLY INDIVIDUALISTIC
    DETERMINATION OF SIN TO A VISION DETERMINED BY THE
    HISTORY OF SALVATION AND THE SOLIDARITY OF SALVATION

In the Bible, the main decision of salvation is the choice between a saving solidarity in Christ and a destructive solidarity in sin. The social aspect of sin is recognized. An individualistic concept of sin that developed in past centuries was culturally conditioned. To a considerable extent it was due to a sacralization and absolutization of those in authority, whether civil or ecclesiastical. They always spoke "in the name of God," and therefore ordinary citizens were allowed no real interest or responsibility in the social, religious, or political realms.

Denied these interests and responsibilities, the average person's interest was directed toward his own salvation alone. We can see an example of this individualistic concept of salvation and sin in the otherwise beautiful book by Thomas à Kempis, *The Imitation of Christ*. The author felt it was sinful to leave his cell and his prayers to be with other people. The Catholic capitalist of the nineteenth century would confess most scrupulously any transgressions of the Eucharistic fast or the Church law for meatless Fridays, and all the small sins of his private life, but it did not occur to him that his activities in the economic realm, which could have brought about terrible suffering to many people, might be enormous sins.

Now, in a world where we so fearfully experience our dependence on one another, and realize that we can save our world only by peaceful coexistence, dialogue, and cooperation, biblical and liturgical renewal draws our attention much more to the Christian's responsibility toward his neighbor, his community, and, indeed, toward the whole of creation. The new science of ecology is but one symbol of the Christian's renewed responsibility for the world around him. Today's Christian is better able to realize that he remains willingly in his sin if he does not join all those men of good will who want to work for a better world, a more brotherly and more personalized molding of all the institutions and structures that affect our life together.

There is a trend of modern thought that studies the environment, public opinion, social prejudice, the heritage, the force of the subconscious, mainly in order to excuse a diminished moral responsibility or to negate the existence of sin. But there is equally a spiritual movement that sees in all these new insights a vigorous challenge and call to responsibility. Each person chooses his own interpretation. If we do not participate actively in the shaping of a healthier public opinion, a healthier way of life—in housing, economic opportunity, and so on—and fail to work to improve our social institutions, we are deciding to remain in our sinfulness and thereby to increase sinfulness in the world. We decidedly remain sinners and relinquish our hope for the Messianic peace if we do not work for reconciliation and peace on all levels. Equally, whoever refuses to his fellow men a proportionate share in responsibility and coresponsibility for the physical, social, cultural, and ecclesiastical life is increasing the sinfulness of the world.

11. The Shift from the Concept of Sin Determined by
    Sanctions and Controls to a Concept Determined by
    Pedagogy and Concern for Development

The kingdom of God becomes visible wherever the disciples of Christ are guided by the Gospel, by mature insight, by love of God, and by the law of grace. Christ wants mature disciples. "I call you servants no longer; a servant does not know what his master is about. I call you friends because I have disclosed to you everything that I have heard from my Father" (Jn. 15:15).

The Church and society have legitimate concerns that made unavoidable a certain amount of control and sanction, particularly where citizens or members of the Church have not reached a certain level of discernment, maturity, and responsibility. However, the control syndrome of authoritarian regimes in Church and state has led to a multiplication of laws and sanctions that hinder the development and maturation of the people under their control. As to the Church, a good example would be a certain approach to worship. There has often been more concern for the uniform performance of all the external cult, for precise control over every public prayer offered, than for education to a worship that would help people to understand the living God and make their whole life an adoration in spirit and truth.

Preoccupation with sacredness, and with control through sacred authority, surrounded everything—rituals, rubrics, vestments, stones—with threats of mortal sin. In a morality determined by the sacredness of authority and of authoritatively proposed norms, the Church's language could speak very easily about a "state of mortal sin." An almost absolute trust in the validity of the juridical norms allowed the constant control and judgment of who might be living in the state of mortal sin.

Let me explain this control by one of the most crucial problems today. A young Catholic lady finds herself, at age eighteen, abandoned by her husband after a few weeks of canonically valid marriage. The whole situation in which the marriage was initiated had given no chance whatsoever for its success. However, under the actual legislation, and in view of particularly scrupulous handling by the marriage tribunal, this first marriage would never be annulled. Years later, this woman marries, knowing that she is disobeying the Church norms but convinced that she has a right to live in normal marriage conditions. Most parish priests of the past generations would have determined uncritically that she was living in a state of mortal sin. At the same time they would have been amazed that a person living in mortal sin could come so regularly to Mass and live such an exemplary family life, giving her children the best possible Christian education.

Today, Church law has been desacralized and a personalistic concern is gaining ground. A new look is emerging. With the more open discussion of good-conscience cases, some people are even wondering if the marriage tribunal itself and those responsible for canon law may be "living in a state of mortal sin" if they refuse to listen to the needs of the faithful. Many theologians would still like to resolve the hard marriage questions by the traditional principle of "invincible ignorance" —that is, that these Catholics do not fully realize that they absolutely have to obey the canonical marriage regulations of the Church. Others, however, pose the question of whether it is the traditionalist canonists who are living in invincible ignorance—or in invincible arrogance. Priests and laymen alike are aware of the sinfulness of unadjusted legislation if no attempt is made to re-examine it honestly. Moreover, they are particularly severe in their judgment of legalistic harshness and insensitivity of mind and heart.

I have already mentioned in a different context the grave consequences of structures and attitudes that mislead many persons to a security neurosis. All this can jeopardize the credibility of the Church and her gospel. On the one hand, there is a clinging to traditions and regulations that alienate many members from the Church while also revealing the separation of religious structures from life and from the needs of the people. On the other hand, we are faced with equally unhealthy reactions against all institutions and laws. This present situation calls for a shift from an ethics of law and obedience to an ethics of responsibility and coresponsibility.

We can argue: Are we not sinning against the living God, the Lord of history, if we try to confront today's new person, shaped by a new culture, with an antiquated concept of sin that was determined primarily by sanctions and concern for external control?

12. THE SHIFT FROM SINS OF DISOBEDIENCE TOWARD SINS AGAINST ONE'S OWN MORAL AUTONOMY

Heteronomy is the enemy of moral maturity. Parents must make many decisions for their children, but they are sinning against the future of their children if they are not aiming, all the while, toward the children's growth and moral maturity. If parents do not allow their children gradually to take the risk of using their own freedom and insight, they are crippling them, stunting their growth, and consequently are guilty of serious sin. They share accountability for a world that suffers from the immaturity of so many people who have not been educated for personal and social responsibility. This applies also to a pastor or confessor who wants to guarantee morality by pressure and sanctions, without respecting the sincere conscience of his fellow Christians. He is sinning against the sacredness of a person's conscience and his right to autonomy.

As modern critical men, we are quite aware that it is not always easy to determine whether sin has been encouraged by the weakness of those in authority who tolerate all kinds of social disorder, or by a system of controls and sanctions that blocks the growth of persons toward maturity and moral autonomy. An erroneous decision can be a great evil, but the greater evil is to deprive human persons of their right to self-determination, by stifling their moral development. Those who want to control the moral behavior of others, without appealing to their consciences and without respecting their right to search sincerely and personally for truth and goodness, belong to the "powers of evil" that are at work in the world.

From a religious point of view, in the light of the New Testament, it is sinful to submit to only external laws instead of acting in view of friendship with God and of the law of grace, in a spirit of gratitude and responsibility for the common good.

Any effort to impose a natural-law concept in an authoritarian way, without joining with all men in shared experience and coreflection about what is good and right, and in order to find authentic solutions to the new problems that arise in the life of individuals and from social relationships, is crippling conscience. To modern man, alienation is a particularly great sin against the God of history and the Redeemer who calls for personal responsibility.

13. THE SHIFT FROM THE LAW TO THE GOSPEL

The law is holy, right, just, good, and even spiritual; it is a gift of the Spirit who renews the face of the earth, if it is framed in the light of the liberating and redeeming action of God. But if it is, in itself, sacralized and absolutized without respect for the good of the person, then it is a killing power and becomes an instrument of depersonalization and of sin. The legalist, and all those who are absolutizing the external order and authority, are depriving law of its force and its footing. They make even the good law a source of sin and misery. Malice, the essence of sin, is unmasked only in the light of the gospel, of the holy, merciful, and redeeming God. As Mary sings with all her life, "His name is Holy; his mercy sure from generation to generation" (Lk. 1:49–50).

In a secular age we can hope to awaken a healthy and saving sense of sin only if we proclaim the gospel and give witness to the God who is holy in his mercy. In the light of the gospel, we see Jansenism and rigorism as destructive sins against God's holiness, which reveals itself in redeeming action. This does not mean that we would tempt people to try to purchase salvation at a discount. Those who take God's redeeming action seriously, and see his holiness manifesting itself in mercy, will combine concern for social justice and mercy. Those who accept the Messianic peace as a gratuitous gift in a spirit of thanksgiving will most generously commit themselves to action for reconciliation, justice, and peace on all levels.

Jansenistic rigorism imposed law violently on others, ignoring the sanction of the gospel that those who are rigorous will be judged by the same measure. There are some who consider themselves as belonging to "the state of perfection" but who keep others rigorously under law without offering them the liberation that manifests itself in the creative serenity of people who live in accordance with God's gracious gifts. They distort the concept and sense of sin, and are themselves sinners against the universal vocation to holiness.

14. The Change of Focus, Owing to the New Emphasis on Religious Liberty and Liberty of Conscience

A wrong sacralization of authority, a perverse objectivism in matters of morality, and a static worldview have produced their bitter fruits in intolerance, in external conformity, and in crimes such as those committed by the Inquisition. In our own time, the minority situation of the whole Christian church, and the horrifying experiences of our generation under Hitler's regime, and under Marxism in various nations, have sharpened our sense of the sinfulness of any form of intolerance. Church institutions, and any Church politics that show more concern for external acceptance than for sincere conscience and loyalty to conscience, come under ever heavier fire. Particularly when external conformity is based on careerism, or on cowardice or selfish expectations, its sinfulness is more easily discerned today than in the past eras of Church regimes.

In everything, including matters of faith and adherence to the Church, today's alert Christians will give prime importance to the whole-hearted search for truth and to sincerity of convictions with the firm intention of putting those convictions into practice. We realize that a man who has not yet come to the fullness of Catholic faith but is open, sincere, and tireless in his search for truth and for truthful action is closer to orthodoxy—that is, to genuine faith that leads to salvation —than one who is clinging to external discipline and formulation without deep convictions. More and more, we see a growing conviction that a "faith that saves" is expressed above all in openness and a search for truth, in dedication to justice, peace, and brotherly love. These are the very signs of a sincere and deep faith. We have become allergic to sins of intolerance and to orthodoxy-without-orthopraxis, and especially allergic to that sinful audacity that asserts something in the name of faith when it is only human tradition.

15. THE CHANGE OF FOCUS IN VIEW OF MODERN ATHEISM

Perhaps the most decisive shift in our concept of sin comes to the foreground in our confrontation with modern atheism. We are no longer satisfied with just condemning it, but rather are looking into the hidden atheism in ourselves and in a number of prejudices even in our institutions and Church structures.

Atheism and secularism force us to examine our consciences about the false image of God that we have conveyed by our wrong concept of sin and our hazardous catalogues of mortal sins. We now know that we have to return to the prophetic tradition in order to realize fully the relation between the concept of sin, or sense of sin, and the knowledge of God or sense of God. More than anything else, a wrong concept of sin can destroy the image of God and make the Church incredible. We have to be ever aware of our mission to make known the message of the holy God, the God of love, truth, and justice, in this critical time.

As an example of what I mean, let us note the attitude of our modern culture and modern states toward the death penalty for crime. Medical research, and deeper insights into certain biological and environmental influences on criminality, and many other things have led several states to abolish the death penalty, or at least not to condemn people too easily to death. The concept of mortal sin is analogous to the death penalty. The sinner is losing eternal life, condemning himself to eternal death; and God will sanction this.

The easy determination of mortal and venial sins, the enormous catalogues of mortal sins based on minutiae, transgressions of sacred traditions, sacred rubrics, and man-made laws, is horrifying when we look at the image of God that this conveys. What does it mean for fostering faith in a God who is love and infinitely more merciful than any modern state, if we so easily assert that, let us say, masturbation by adolescents, or by adults who have serious difficulties in overcoming the habit, is "mortal sin"? If no human judge today would dare to condemn an eleven- or twelve-year-old to jail for a lifetime, how can we, in our judgments, threaten them with jail for all eternity?

I am extremely happy that the encyclical of Paul VI on human life, *Humanae Vitae,* did not repeat a previous doctrinal assertion that the use of any contraceptive is to be considered an objectively grave [mortal] sin even in a situation where responsible transmission of life is not possible. Rigoristic moral teaching can terribly sharpen the crisis of faith, especially when it concentrates on matters in which specialists in other fields are more competent than ministers of the Church. This holds even more if the rigorists, whose task should be to be witnesses to the gospel, fail to take seriously the poverty and humility of service most clearly requested by it.

About ten years ago, a group of very dedicated students at a Roman state university asked me to speak to them on

moral theology as a source of unbelief. The very request was
a shock to me. However, I finally agreed to think about this
question. Indeed, the crisis of faith forces us to deepen our
own faith and to avoid any statement about sin, and especially
about mortal sin, that would convey a wrong image of God.
This, however, must be said not only against rigorism but
equally against that laxism that practically presents God as an
old grandfather who nods "yes, yes" to whatever nonsense or
dangerous attitudes the children want to indulge in.

The crisis of faith is teaching us to be extremely cautious
about proposing man-made norms and catalogues of sin in the
name of God. Furthermore, we have to ask ourselves in the
community of faith if certain norms given in the Bible are
truly meant for all ages and cultures. At the same time, we
must take much more seriously the sins against the goal commandments, against those orientations that call us to the gratitude, generosity, and creative action that is the fitting response
to the gospel.

2

Sin as Alienation and Sins of Alienation

Over the past decades, biblical scholars have warned us time and again that we cannot understand the biblical message on sin and conversion unless we consider each individual writer and each book of the Old and New Testaments in its historical context. Each statement on sin has its *sitz im leben*. It is never abstract and timeless but is always integrated into the concrete message of salvation that calls man to conversion at a certain historical moment.[1] Were we to ignore the historical context of the biblical message or of the magisterium's past teachings on sin, our discourse on the subject would be an alienation from history, from life, and thus from the God of history.

In fidelity to the Bible, we can speak of sin only with our eyes on the *kairos*, the actual situation in which we are called to conversion, and in a readiness to accuse ourselves of our sins. Any discussion and theologizing about sin, its origin and its essence, that in practice leads us to self-justification or to flight from reality is an alienation from God and from our human vocation. "A right concern for this topic of sin cannot

1. Rudolf Schnackenburg, *Christian Existence in the New Testament*, Vol. 1 (Notre Dame, Ind.: University of Notre Dame Press, 1968), pp. 221–28.

inspire us to speculate on sin's origin but only to confess our guilt."[2]

To talk about sin and conversion from sin in an era of atheism and secularism means coming to grips with the Marxist and secularist accusation that religion alienates from life. Although the point must be made that genuine faith is the very opposite of alienation, I believe that the accusation itself presents us with a key concept for a proper understanding of sin: *alienation.*

Sin is total alienation from God, from faith, from adoration, from knowledge of God, and from our fellow men. This is, in a very striking sense, the sin of atheism and secularism, which often are reactions against religions, churches, and so-called pious people who themselves are alienated from God or have no real knowledge of him, and whose talk on sin is therefore, to a great extent, alienating. The Marxist accusation was an unjust generalization which, unfortunately, created still more alienation; but it is a fact that many forms of atheism and secularism represent the estrangement of a son who, in his hostility toward an unfriendly father, cannot break out of the vicious circle of alienation.

I have written in other books[3] about the strengths and weaknesses of Karl Marx's philosophy and doctrine. Here I need only say that his vision remains paradoxical and conflicting. He was right about the manipulation of the common man by the alienated, profit-oriented infrastructures of the economic process, but he was wrong in teaching that all religion or faith in God is a produce of those structures, and that a battle against faith in God and adoration of God is necessary for man's liberation. Precisely the opposite is true:

2. G. C. Berkouwer, *Sin* (Grand Rapids, Mich.: Wm. B. Eerdmans, 1971), p. 65; see p. 40.

3. Among others: *A Theology of Protest* (New York: Farrar, Straus & Giroux, 1970), pp. xiii, 10, 50, 80, 172. Also: *Morality Is for Persons* (New York: Farrar, Straus & Giroux, 1971), pp. 62–68, 78.

It is faith in God and adoration of God that is necessary for the liberation of man.

Marx was a victim of his own scientific socialism and dialectic materialism; he could not envisage the conversion of man's heart as the absolute condition of all structural changes. At heart he was a moralist in the Israeli tradition of his own ancestry, but he could not affirm, and indeed emphatically denied, any relevance of an ethical approach to the great problems of life. In a kind of scientific alchemy, he expected a historically necessary final liberation and harmony; but the base metals he chose for transmutation were class hatred and class struggle. He was like a wrathful prophet in view of the exploitation of the poor, yet at the same time he held that an ever-increasing accumulation of wealth in the hands of the exploiters, with correspondingly growing misery of the working class, is the basic dialectic law of history and must, therefore, not be counteracted by gradual reforms.

The great alienation of Marxism and of modern organized atheism and secularism, however, is estrangement from God. Such disjunction is not new; it stems from the total alienation in the world, which is the bitter fruit of all sins of mankind. To a great extent it represents a reaction to such other forms of alienation as unholy worldliness and the equally unholy unworldliness that is so deeply rooted in many forms of organized religion, including Christianity (cf. *GS*, 19). Militant atheism, which finds its most organized form in Marxism, is the disastrous fulfillment of those forms of alienation.

Papini's famous book, *The Devil*, can probably be regarded as a parody on the dialectic alchemy of Marxism, which hopes that final liberation and peace will emerge from growing hatred and tensions among the social classes. Papini follows the devils, who are unreservedly devoted to the development of their heritage, and from day to day learn new forms of malice and hatred. But when they come to the point of having nothing more to add or to learn, they suddenly convert and become peaceful penitents before God.

The Holy Office, which forbade Catholic bookstores to distribute the book, apparently did not understand the underlying wit. Surely Papini was not so naïve as to believe that schooling in malice and increasing alienation in sin would be proper preparation for conversion. The more man becomes estranged from God and falls into the slavery of sin, the more difficult and improbable conversion becomes. Growing hatred and violence will never produce genuine peace and nonviolent commitment. For all believers, the ultimate alienation that we find in atheism and secularism becomes a loud call to overcome all the many forms of alienation, a call to an unconditional return to God, not in an abstract spiritualism but in a common action for gradual liberation and a general reconciliation in all the dimensions of our existence.

It seems to me, then, that the concept of alienation could be a key concept for a theology of sin and a call to individual and collective conversion not only from the seductive influences of secularism and atheism but also from the polarizations fostered by an alienated traditionalism and a careless horizontalism.

1. Refusal to Know and to Adore God

In a perspective that defines sin in terms of actual deliberation and awareness, one might think that the atheist or the secularist who has closed his mind to the thought of God would no longer be able to commit sin. The decisive dimension—offense of God—does not come to his conscious awareness. His moral failures would then be understood only as contradiction to human development and disturbance in the ordering of human life. On the contrary, what I assert here is that atheism and secularism are the most complete embodiments of sinfulness and manifest the deepest roots of sin, insofar as the loss of the sense of sin and manifold disorders and alienations are a result of the refusal of the atheist or the secularist to know and to adore God. However, in saying this,

I do not pass judgment on any individual person but seek only to analyze the whole human phenomenon in the light of the Bible and the signs of the time.

A person's decisive moral and religious choice lies in whether or not he wants to know God ever more, and honor him who is the origin, center, and goal of our life. Today we are not interested in theoretical discussions and assertions of the existence or nonexistence of God as "a higher being" or "prime cause" or whatever, if this has nothing to do with the ordering of man's life. We are primarily concerned with the refusal to adore God and to know him insofar as worship is part of the living enterprise.

St. Paul, in his letter to the Romans, throws a brilliant light on this whole theme. He asserts clearly and emphatically that the refusal to know God and to render thanks to him constitutes the source of all alienation, since it perverts man himself and disturbs his relationship to his neighbor and environment. The great sin comes from refusal of that truth that gives meaning to all human life: "For we see divine retribution revealed from heaven and falling upon all the godless wickedness of men. In their wickedness they are stifling the truth. For all that may be known of God by men lies plain before their eyes; indeed God himself has disclosed it to them. His invisible attributes, that is to say his everlasting power and deity, have been visible ever since the world began, to the eye of reason, in the things he has made. There is therefore no possible defense for their conduct; knowing God, they have refused to honor him as God, or to render him thanks. Hence all their thinking has ended in futility, and their misguided minds are plunged in darkness. They boast of their wisdom, but they have made fools of themselves. . . . For this reason, God has given them up to the vileness of their own desires, and the consequent degradation of their bodies, because they have bartered away the true God for a false one, and have offered reverence and worship to created things instead of to the Creator, who is blessed for ever; amen. In consequence, I say, God has given them up to shameful passions. . . . Thus, because they have not seen fit to acknowledge God, he has given them up to their own depraved reason. This leads them to break all rules of conduct. They are filled with every kind of injustice, mischief, rapacity, and malice. . . . They show no loyalty to parents, no conscience, no fidelity to their plighted word. . . . Not only so, they actually applaud such practices" (Rom. 1:18–32). The words "they have not seen fit to acknowledge God" specifically express the alienation into which secularism is plunged. It is the refusal of that knowledge of God that is existential acknowledgment. Secularism seems to be even more alienated from God than some forms of atheism where a man still remains tied to the question of God. The emphatic objection against religions is a sign that he has not yet fully come to the point of silencing his desire to search for God. On the contrary, the typical, complete secularist has reached that total alienation where there is no longer any yearning to search for the ultimate meaning of life or to return to friendship with a personal God.

The epistle to the Romans presents a commentary on the first chapters of the book of Genesis. Early in human history, the great alienation begins with the monologue of man. He hides himself from God through his alienating concern for self-enhancement, self-determination, and wisdom for his own glory. He refuses to acknowledge the gratuitous gift of God in all that man possesses and can do. Through its own literary genre, Genesis demonstrates the immediate and grave consequences of this alienation from God. It renders man a stranger unto himself and seriously disturbs his rapport with his neighbor and the world about him. The man who refuses to adore God seeks domination over his neighbor and even over his marriage partner, sexual relationships included. "Man shall dominate over you" (Gen. 3:16).

Atheism and secularism become a program of life where those who have refused to acknowledge and adore the living

God attempt to manipulate and to exploit others, to use them as objects, thus casting themselves in the role of false gods. All forms of manipulation of one's fellow men are incarnations of that alienation that begins with a refusal to honor God and to honor man as the image and likeness of God.

A man who does not consider God worthy of being recognized or adored inevitably chooses a chaos of values. His whole life and personal relationships are disturbed by this fundamental alienation. "Then, not content with gross error in their knowledge of God, men live in the constant warfare of ignorance and call this monstrous evil peace. They perform ritual murders of children and secret ceremonies and the frenzied orgies of unnatural cults; the purity of life and marriage is abandoned; and a man treacherously murders his neighbor or corrupts his wife and breaks his heart. All is in chaos—bloody murder, theft and fraud, corruption, treachery, riot, perjury, honest men driven to distraction; ingratitude, moral corruption, sexual perversion, breakdown of marriage, adultery, debauchery. For the worship of idols, whose names it is wrong even to mention, is the beginning, cause and end of every evil. . . . They have thought wrongly about God, because in their contempt for religion, they have deliberately perjured themselves. It is not any power in what they swear by, but the nemesis of sin, that always pursues the transgression of the wicked" (Wis. 14:22–31).

In spite of all the compromises of theologians who go too far with a certain type of secularization, I firmly hold to the concept that sin is an offense against God, an injustice toward the Creator and Father, a refusal of his friendship. The death of Christ manifests to us this horrifying aspect of sin. However, we must insist equally on the other aspect, namely, that sin damages most of all the sinner himself and the world around him. The sinner falls into the slavery and alienation of sinfulness. He becomes a temptation to his neighbor and a source of alienation to his total environment.

The man who does not adore the true God is, of necessity,

building his own idols. He becomes a self-worshiper and is enslaved to many false ideologies, for instance that of using truth for self-aggrandizement, and he becomes increasingly blind as he distances himself from the light. Sin is truly directed against the holiness of God, it is a refusal of God's right to be adored with one's whole being and life.

The offense against the holiness of God is also expressed in the attitude of those who do not want to recognize their own need of conversion and redemption or who, in their own self-importance, do not seek the redeeming and sanctifying action of the holy God. The self-righteous and proud man denies the honor due to God, and in turn deprives himself of the salvation offered by God.

"Salvation" is not at all an exclusively supernatural concept. It implies also liberation, healing, and homecoming to God in one's existential wholeness. We shall see later how the rejection of salvation, the gift of the holy God, entails nonacceptance of one's personal integration and the forfeiture of one's own wholeness. It stands as a repudiation of one's proper place in the world and thus becomes a decision for complete alienation.

Where the Scriptures speak of sin, both aspects are always equally emphasized. The sinner's alienation when he abandons God results from his injustice toward God in denying him adoration and rejecting a life in the Covenant with him. "Hark you heavens, and earth give ear, for the Lord has spoken: I have sons whom I reared and brought up, but they have rebelled against me. The ox knows its owner and the ass its master's stall; but Israel, my own people, has no knowledge, no discernment. O sinful nation, people loaded with iniquity, race of evildoers, wanton destructive children who have deserted the Lord, spurned the Holy One of Israel and turned your backs on him. . . . Your head is covered with sores, your body diseased. . . . Your country is desolate, your cities lie in ashes" (Is. 1:2–7).

In this passage, Isaiah indicates the whole theme of his

book: Because Israel has neglected the Holy One, the nation and all those who are responsible for it find themselves in dereliction and alienation. Of their own choice, they prepare themselves for exile, the great symbol of total alienation. "Two sins have my people committed: They have forsaken me, a spring of living water, and they have hewn out for themselves cisterns, cracked cisterns that can hold no water" (Jer. 2:13). The two sins are here shown in their oneness; the second sin is the unavoidable result of the first, namely, of forsaking the spring of living water. The prophets are very explicit about this: "Is it not your desertion of the Lord your God that brings all this upon you? . . . It is your own wickedness that will punish you, your own apostasy that will condemn you" (Jer. 2:17–19). The injustice to God appears particularly grave, because all that Israel and the sinner are gaining by their refusal of adoration is alienation and misery (cf. Jer. 16:11, 17:3; Baruch 3:12; I Sam. 8:8; I Kings 19:10).

The earlier quoted text of the epistle to the Romans stresses the grave injustice of those who do not render thanks. This constitutes also one of the main themes of the prophetic discourse on sin, particularly in Deuteronomy. Since the Covenant is an undeserved gift of God, to abide in the Covenant and gratefully fulfill its conditions in constant praise of God means salvation; to refuse it is misery. Moral disorder unmasks a person's lack of gratitude. "Jacob ate and was well-fed, Jeshurun grew fat and unruly, he grew fat, he grew bloated and sleek. He forsook God who made him and dishonored the Rock of his salvation. You forsook the creator who begot you and cared nothing for God who brought you to birth. The Lord saw and spurned them; his own sons and daughters provoked him. 'I will hide my face from them,' he said; 'let me see what their end will be'" (Deut. 32:15–20).

A discourse on sin that one-sidedly emphasizes the loss of sanctifying grace seems far removed from a full biblical understanding of sin. Surely the most frightful thing is to lose friendship with God, a loss that involves the person in his total orientation and innermost being. He loses his direction and becomes thoroughly alienated, and not only on a supernatural level. Since he does not consider God worthy of acknowledgment, he gradually sinks into all kinds of disorder, pitting himself against the whole reality of God and his creation, including himself. If not all the dreadful consequences of this loss of God's friendship become evident, it is because of man's own limitations. His decision may not represent a total alienation from God, since he lacked the necessary awareness.

Secularism is not always a complete and irreversible choice. As outsiders we can never judge the human person who lapses into a secularistic attitude. God alone knows the extent to which a person has rejected him with the quality of choice that involves all levels of the human being. It might well be that a man who considers himself a secularist, and whom others consider to be one, may have rejected only a closed system of religious thought while being already on the road to transcend himself in openness to others for the common good, and thus he may be sincerely searching for God.

The disastrous consequences of sin against God—that refusal to acknowledge God and to render him thanks—can be understood and exemplified in what Viktor Frankl calls "noogenic neurosis."[4] The spiritual emptiness of a person not existentially seeking the meaning of his life causes countless mental and bodily disturbances. This type of neurosis, which is one of the most striking signs of deep alienation, cannot be healed unless the person sincerely begins to seek the ultimate meaning and purpose of his life.

If we speak of the refusal to acknowledge God, our discourse cannot remain at the level of abstract knowledge; it has to impart that knowledge which gives direction to life and involves the whole man. Only the person who sets out to pursue, in an existential way, the knowledge of God who is love can transcend himself in authentic love.

4. Bernard Häring, *Medical Ethics* (Notre Dame, Ind.: Fides, 1973), pp. 168–69, 173–75, 194–96.

The full malice of refusal to know and to acknowledge God is seen in those who have had the opportunity to know the living God and to welcome Jesus Christ, the sacrament of God's own love on earth, but who, either because of their self-justification by law or their sacred egotism as individuals or groups, refuse to acknowledge him. Christ points an accusing finger at them: "You know neither me nor my Father; if you knew me you would know my Father as well" (Jn. 8:19). Instead of seeking liberation from their self-concern, they have locked themselves inside their own egotism. If they call God their father, they are liars. And Jesus responds, "If God were your father, you would love me, for God is the source of my being, and from him I come. I have not come of my own accord; he sent me. . . . Your father is the devil and you choose to carry out your father's desires. . . . There is no truth in him. When he tells a lie he is speaking his own language" (Jn. 8:42–44).

In a world saturated with secularism and materialism, not all people have the same opportunity to know God. Therefore it would sometimes seem advisable to use a terminology in keeping with their secular culture and say that whoever, by his own egotism, consciously or implicitly refuses to seek the ultimate meaning of his life cannot truly know himself and cannot share in authentic relationships with others. Wherever a man is truly seeking genuine relationships with others and is breaking out of his self-centeredness, he is already on the way in his search for the knowledge of God.

Although today's world precludes our passing judgment on individual persons, God's judgment on a mankind that refuses knowledge of his design remains always valid. "Not to know and acknowledge God is not an error but guilt."[5] True knowledge of God comes as a response to God's bounties and his appeal, and is the privilege of a man who is and becomes ever more able to love. Gratitude for his gifts becomes

5. Rudolf Bultmann, *Theology of the New Testament* (London: SCM Press, 1951), Vol. 1, pp. 314–16.

love of his will. "To know God and his name means to acknowledge him, render him glory, submit oneself to his
will."[6]

The true knowledge of God means almost the same as holy
fear of God. It is an awe so profound that only adoration
and the honoring of God by the truthfulness of one's life can
be one's response. Man's unwillingness to know God and to
love his holy will is a radical sin because he is in no way ready
to love anyone (cf. Rom. 3:16; Is. 59:8; Heb. 3:10).

Basic pride and truthlessness are the chief reasons why the
world did not recognize God when he came among his own
(Jn. 1:10–11). Whoever dwells in his pride and trusts his own
wisdom makes himself unable to know and to acknowledge
God's wisdom (I Cor. 1:21). A conversion to God's reality
always includes the fundamental readiness to embrace truth
as one's orientation to life (I Tim. 2:4; Tit. 1:1; Heb. 10:26).
Only those who accept the gift and command to love their
brethren can be true adorers of God (cf. I Jn. 3:1 and 4:6).
Each discrete step toward a greater knowledge of God therefore involves a growing liberation from self-centeredness and
a fuller conversion to the love of God and of one's neighbor.
"This is eternal life: to know thee who alone art truly God,
and Jesus Christ whom thou has sent" (Jn. 17:3).

2. ALIENATION OF CULT AND OF DOCTRINE

Classical treatises on the virtue of religion differentiated
specifically and totally between the cult of false gods and a
false cult of the true God. In relation to the message of the
Bible and the experience of life, the distinction is not as clear
as that. It is quite possible for a person participating in the
Christian liturgy to be, in his heart, more godless and more
alienated from God than one who calls himself an atheist or
a secularist. The latter could be gradually opening himself to

6. Ibid., Vol. 1, p. 316. *Theology of the New Testament*, New York:
Scribner's, Vol. 1, 1951; Vol. 2, 1955.

the other in victory over his self-centeredness and thus be on the road that brings him to the knowledge of God.

I do not approach the unworthy and alienating cult in the perspective of the virtue of religion; the treatment of virtue in the manuals of the immediate past considered mainly the virtuousness of the individual person and therefore did not organically lead to the social and communitarian aspects of cult. Our present treatment of *asebeia*, that is, of the alienation from adoration, is taken not only as a lack of individual virtue but also as an objective phenomenon, as the sum of all the alienations and faults of worship and gratitude toward God. It is an alienation that gradually shapes the whole orientation of individuals and of whole groups and communities.[7]

Since my scope is totally different from that of manuals destined for confessors and penitents, I shall keep an eye on the whole political horizon—the structures and social motivations that are a part and a cause of alienation from God.

Wherever religion and cult serve as means for conserving a certain political or social order in support of a privileged class, alienation creeps into the whole phenomenon of religion, including liturgy. This is particularly the case where the state uses religion and cult for self-glorification. This danger threatens not only pagan religions and the pagan state but has also tremendously damaged Christianity whenever and wherever the Church became predominantly a Church of the empire and sought her security in sacred alliances between throne and altar.

The most striking phenomenon of alienation in the field of cult and doctrine has come from a type of sacralization which, through a wrong concept of the sacred, contradicts and darkens the revelation of the holy God. One realizes that reverence before the holy God and consequent care for a worthy

---

7. Cf. L. Köhler, *Theologie des Altan Testament* (Tübingen, 1936), pp. 160–61. The American translation of this work is *Old Testament Theology* (Philadelphia: Westminster Press, 1957). Also cf. K. Föster, "Sebomai, Eusebeia, Asebeia" in *Theologische Wörterbuch zum Neuen Testament* VII, pp. 168–90.

cult grant a certain sacredness to forms that guarantee dignity in the cult. But wherever faith is weakened, there is a human tendency to sacralize laws and rubrics surrounding the cult, in such a way that the ritual itself becomes the goal. I have already indicated the danger that lurks in sacralizing human traditions in a way that opposes them to the divinely revealed truth. An undue emphasis given these traditions can obscure the doctrine of faith: "This people pays me lip-service but their heart is far from me; their worship of me is in vain, for they teach as doctrines the commandments of men" (Mt. 15:8–9). Alienation of liturgy and alienation of doctrine go hand in hand; they interpenetrate. The Pharisees and scribes, and some of their modern counterparts—theologians, canonists, specialists in religion—become such meticulous specialists that they practically lose genuine knowledge of God, and veil his countenance. Thus their estrangement becomes worse than that of the prostitutes and tax-gatherers.

There is a kind of scrupulosity in matters of rubrics and traditions that is practically a defensive compensation mechanism. Behind the scrupulous observance and compulsive accuracy in obedience to minutiae, the alienated person wants to hide from himself and others his real lack of faith. So it was that the priestly class of the Pharisees became a godless world hermetically sealed from the appeal of grace and the prayer of Christ, and for which Jesus no longer prayed (Jn. 14:19, 17:9).

The sin and alienation of the churchman who dispenses God's judgments and charisms as if he were their proprietor is worse than the crudest superstitions and primitive beliefs in magic. Such a specialist in religion has closed his mind and heart to the suffering and needs of his neighbor, especially the humble people. He manipulates both the concept and the expression of the sacred, and the cult thus stands as an alienated religious world under the judgment of God. He has become unable to welcome and to follow the Son of God with that knowledge that is the fruit and source of the filial love of

God and concern for neighbor (cf. Jn. 12:31, 15:10, 16:8–11). The prophets, to whom was granted the sense of the holy God, sharply denounced such cultish alienation from the holy God and from neighborly love. "Because this people approach me with their mouths and honor me with their lips, while their hearts are far from me and their religion is but a precept of men, learnt by rote; therefore I will yet again shock this people, adding shock to shock: the wisdom of their wise men shall vanish and the discernment of the discerning shall be lost" (Is. 29:13–14). The text refers especially to that strange casuistry about the cult that obscures the gifts and call of God.

The history of religions, including that of the chosen people and of Christian churches, records numerous instances of almost incredible alienation from the sacred. False sacralization of rituals and doctrines led not only to a loss of dynamism toward a life in justice and love but became a real barrier, blinding man to his moral vocation. "Their heart is far from me; their worship of me is in vain. . . . How well you set aside the commandment of God in order to maintain your tradition! Moses said, 'Honor your father and your mother' and 'the man who curses his father or mother must suffer death.' But you hold that if a man says to his father and mother, 'Anything of mine which might have been used for your benefit is *corban* [meaning, set apart for God], he is no longer permitted to do anything for his father and mother. Thus by your own tradition, handed down among you, you make God's word null and void" (Mk. 7:7–13).

The alienating decay within the liturgy during the past centuries can best be understood as part of this whole phenomenon of alienation. Two very striking examples will illustrate this: the mass said by choice in private as the explicit rejection of the community celebration, and a widespread legalistic and individualistic presentation of the sacrament of penance. The way the Eucharist was understood and celebrated, and the one-sided emphasis on auricular confession in a prescribed setting, have justly been viewed by historians as alienation from community and thus from the Covenant.[8]

Romano Guardini held that a liturgy alienated from life and from the sense of the holy and living God can be a source of defection of the masses. Many modern liturgists and others who are concerned to bring the liturgy home to its original simplicity and vitality echo his view. They feel that the clinging of some people and groups to an alienated liturgy is, in reality, a sign of their practical lack of faith and possibly of a hidden atheism.

In spite of the difficulties in the liturgical field today, it would be altogether unjust to accuse the liturgy itself of alienation. There is only partial alienation in some sectors of the Church. However, it is not too bold to say that many pages of manuals of moral theology and of rubricism have shown a shockingly alienated and alienating concept of the sacred. Some assumed the use of the "sacred language"—Latin —to be more important than communication of the language of joy. Concern for uniformity, and insistence on rigorous control of everything, are signs of profound alienation from the creative experience of human life and of true adoration. Such alienating concepts and performance of liturgy have done more to impede than to foster adoration of God in spirit and truth.

A cult alienated from life and from true adoration is usually the outcome of an erroneous concept of the sacred and consequently of the sacred-profane dichotomy, combined with a wrong sacralization of a priestly class that jealously guards its monopoly of initiation. Alienation in worship resulted from excessive concern for sacred privileges and sacred power.[9] Since the laity was considered "profane," it could not be fully initiated into worship and could not fully participate in the services. The exclusion of women from the

8. C. Vogel, "An Alienated Liturgy" in *Concilium* VIII (February 1972), pp. 11–25.

9. Bernard Häring, *Faith and Morality in the Secular Age* (Garden City, N.Y.: Doubleday, 1973).

sanctuary, and the many other prescriptions discriminating against them in the past (and now) have also resulted from a mentality that viewed women as impure and profane.

Even in doctrine and dogma, wrong sacralizations can lead to a dangerous alienation. The keynote of the revealed doctrine is liberation and salvation for all people, a joyous proclamation of the salvation message, and concelebration of the mystery of faith. But as legalism grew, the main perspective became not so much communication and witness of faith as ecclesiastical control by formalists who often were intolerant of other cultural groups whom they suspected of heresy. Despite even the Second Vatican Council's reinstatement of the perspective and tone of proclamation and witness, and its emphasis on these the already famous project of a *Lex Fundamentalis*, "the fundamental law" elaborated by the Canon Law Commission, has reverted to the teaching of doctrine from the standpoint of control. Control supersedes proclamation and witness.

In addition to the legalism and power of Canon Law, there have been alienating influences also in the field of doctrine. I refer especially to the militant spirit within the Christian churches and particularly within the various theological schools. If members of some religious orders were to receive permission to teach doctrine, they had to swear a solemn oath to defend the tradition of their school. In debate this often resulted in a greater emphasis on narrow fidelity to their traditions than to the central themes of the history of salvation. An extreme conceptualism came to identify the human concept with the mystery toward which it is pointing. The practical results came close to a negation of the ineffable mystery of the infinite God.

In all honesty, it must be admitted that numerous heresies did arise that threatened orthodox teaching, but often enough the accusations masked a security complex that attributed too much importance to the identity of specific formulas. Obviously, there was a lack of awareness that each formulation is time-bound and can be read only in its own historical context. The very desire to repeat continually the same formulations not only diminishes the joy and dynamism of faith but endangers the real identity of the message itself.

3. The Alienation of Israel and of Church Institutions

Yahweh chose for the Covenant a poor and miserable nation, a group of uneducated tribes, to manifest his goodness and to glorify his graciousness to man. But often in its history, Israel was ungrateful for the undeserved gift of the revelation and the Covenant, even to the point of using it as a reason for contemptuous pride before other nations, although in God's design Israel should have been servant and witness to the one God before all nations. Its self-sacralization caused many divisions as the cult of Yahweh became gradually the expression of an arrogant nation. This is probably the meaning of the cult of the golden calf (Ex. 32). It may have represented an orgiastic cult through which Israel wanted to celebrate its own divine forces as a privileged nation rather than to give itself humbly to the Lord and to the witness of the one God through service and solidarity. In refusing to serve gratefully for the gift of the law and the Covenant, Israel became entangled in the conflicts of other superpowers that also had traditionally sacralized their collective pride and selfishness. Thus Israel became more and more involved in the alienation of the tribes and kingdoms in the neighboring regions.

The false sacralizations of Israel, the superficial and eccentric life of its priestly class, and especially the arrogance of the nation, led to its rejecting the Messiah when finally he came to his own. In the influential circles of the priests, Pharisees, and scribes, the expectation was of a Messiah who would enhance the nation's glory and serve the sacralized groups. Indeed, even those called by the Lord to his discipleship also were tainted by this aberrant hope (cf. Mt. 16:22–23).

The misguided Messianic hope has been perpetuated in the

many individual and collective sins of the Church, in its triumphalism, in the Crusades, in intolerance, and in sacred alliances between throne and altar. All were under the cover of sacred pretexts that served the egotism of princes and privileged classes as well as of the so-called "higher clergy."

Along the same lines of alienation was the warped trust in the *brachium seculare*, the secular state which, by sanctions and promises, could guarantee unity in one faith in submission to the hierarchy. Often the result was more external uniformity than faith. The mixture of concern for the orthodox faith (*fides quae*), and a distorted sacralization of power, tended to damage sincere adherence to faith (*fides qua*). The bitter harvest came in the form of hypocrisy, ecclesiastical careerism, and innumerable sins of simony. The Church, including monasteries with men under the vow of poverty, all too often became a *brachium mortuum*, an establishment that would receive inheritances of earthly goods and privileges but would give no thought to reciprocating.

A sacralization that was probably more alienating than any other was the arrogated power of the Pope ("Church") over the secular sphere. This led to a thousand forms of unholy unworldliness. The more recent theory of the indirect power of the Church over the temporal sphere can be rightly understood, but it became and still stands as an alienating sacralization. Especially is this the case when the emphasis is on the power dimension. The proclamation of doctrine and moral imperatives then becomes linked more to the exercise of this power than to a humble witness to the gospel.

It cannot be denied that these sins were common occurrences and became increasingly more apparent in the ecclesiastical structures and language. Wherever this happens, the world holds well-founded suspicions of the clergy's intentions, and the Church and her ministry lose their credibility instead of becoming always and everywhere humble proclamations of God's kingdom. The faithful and the world at large are led to question whether those who proclaim the gospel and moral imperatives truly want only to serve God or are trying to confuse God's kingdom with their own desire to dominate others, to impose their earthly and self-serving concepts of morality and order.

The alliance between throne and altar led to countless alienating sacralizations in the way authority was exercised by both the Church and the secular princes. The Church became a sacred monarchy, bishops imitated the sovereignty of the kings and princes, and all too often a corrupt monarchy received protection from the sacred realm. In this unhealthy situation, the Church of the state, with its diplomatic corps, the Pope, the Curia, and the bishops, often resembled the ancient Israelites in their involvement in this world's political contests. Due to this, she lost to a considerable extent her prophetic role.

One of the inevitable consequences can be discerned in the many forms of alienation that developed within the Canon Law of the Church. Very often it severed itself from the gospel, from the whole people of God, and from the prime mission of the Church to proclaim the gospel and give witness to it.

This whole sad picture was produced by the cumulative sins of individuals, of groups, of communities, and of regimes. One of their capital sins was in not crying out to God for prophets and in not listening to them when they were sent. The alienation in the structures and in the whole environment incited to innumerable sins of cowardice and of external hypocritical conformity. Whenever we stop to consider our own conversion and the reform of Church structures for the fulfillment of her mission in the world, we must have firmly in mind all of this complex phenomenon.

4. ALIENATION IN THE FIELD OF ASCETICS AND THE STYLE OF DEVOTIONS

The alienation of the clergy and ritualism alienated from the mainstreams of life had a negative influence on popular devotions and on the whole concept of ascetical life. Forms of prayer proper to the monks, who had withdrawn from life, gradually became the ideal on which everyone was to model himself. Control over orthodoxy was extended to all preformulated prayers, so that no prayer could be said publicly without previous approval. Thus many never dared to express themselves in spontaneous prayer; even their individual prayer was limited to the recitation of formulas that had arisen in contexts totally different from their own.

A shocking symptom of all this alienation in prayer was that nuns, particularly those under papal enclosure in the Latin Church, were obliged to recite their breviary in the Latin language although most were not of the Latin culture and had no knowledge of the language. Other prayers, too, had to be said in Latin. The requirement that the diocesan clergy had to use the breviary used in the monastic life shows the same trend in prayer life: one totally alienated from the life context in which the person should "adore God in spirit and truth."

A disincarnate verticalism and the formalism of devotion and prayers reflected the partial alienation of the priestly class and of ecclesiastical institutions. The whole picture somehow explains why so many parts of the Church silenced for a long time the prophetic voices that brought discomfort and disquiet. Prophets grow up in a prayer life that brings them truly in contact with the living God and helps them to realize his presence in the events of human history. We can probably hypothesize that the security complex so deeply rooted in the sacralized institutions is a built-in obstacle to the personal and communitarian prayer that can lead to the prophetic experience of the holy God. Unconsciously, the prisoners of false security are protecting themselves from prophets who would make them uncomfortable. This is the defensive mechanism inherent in the situation.

But today's reaction against a disincarnate spiritualism, verticalism, and lifeless forms of prayer, spiritual exercises and penance rituals that were rooted in so many other alienations, may itself be yielding to equally alienating forms of horizontalism, materialism, and secularism. Having been confronted with only the former type of piety and asceticism, even well-intentioned persons find—at least temporarily—little or no meaning in a life of prayer. However, what they are rejecting is not always prayer itself but an alienated and alienating form of prayer.

It seems to me that the decisive step in overcoming the many forms of estrangement that have crept into ecclesiastical institutions, Canon Law, and the law's application, is first and foremost a renewal of prayer according to the prophetic tradition of the Old Testament and of the great prophets of church history: men like St. Francis and St. Dominic. I include also St. Alphonsus of Liguori who, through his numerous spiritual writings, exerted a tremendous force against rigorism and Jansenism. His influence stemmed from his characteristically spontaneous prayers and the spiritual formation he promoted for creativity and spontaneity in prayer.

A profound renewal of prayer and of the sacrament of reconciliation, which eliminates the alienating aspects of individualism, formalism, and ritualism, can counteract both the old verticalism and the equally dangerous new horizontalism. The widespread movement of "houses of prayer" promotes renewal of prayer in total trust in the Spirit and fosters a style of prayer that is more personal, closer to life, and watchful of the signs of the times. Prayer is becoming what it should be, a personal and communal expression of faith that brings life home to God.[10]

5. ALIENATION OF MORAL THEOLOGY AND THE CONCEPT OF SIN

Estrangement derives its power from defective institutions and from an immature life of persons. Its effects permeate also

10. Bernard Häring, *Faith and Morality in the Secular Age* (Garden City, N.Y.: Doubleday, 1973). See Chapter 7, "Renewal of Prayer in a Secular Age." Sister Mary McDevitt, I.H.M., "Journal of House of Prayer" in *Studia Moralis* (Rome: Academia Alfonsiana, 1971), pp. 283–98.

the approaches and teachings of moral theology and philosophical ethics. Indeed, the teaching of morality in many major seminaries and in various catechisms often mirror the alienation that has filtered down into institutions and the hearts of men.

If I address myself here to moral theology and morals, I want to caution against generalizations. We should not forget that the moral message is transmitted to us not only by the specialists who have taught moral theology and interpreted laws. The mainstream of tradition is the message that saints have written by their own lives and by their witness. Furthermore, in the Catholic tradition of moral theology, there have always been courageous efforts to overcome alienation in all its forms.

The following section aims to unmask the sinful concept of sin, which is the consequence of alienation in various complex expressions of moral theology.

(a) *The moral message alienated from the celebration of the sacred mysteries*

The secularist is a man who has no interest in the knowledge of God and thus refuses to adore him. This is the most radical alienation of man from the holy God. This process begins within the moral teaching itself when moral norms and imperatives "gain" independence from the mystery of God and celebration of the mysteries in the sacraments of Christ. We have already seen to what extent the concept and the administration of the sacraments became alienated from their original dynamism by rituals that were no longer rooted in life experience and therefore failed to communicate the message of life. It comes as no surprise, then, that manuals of moral theology approached the sacraments one-sidedly in the perspective of precepts and commandments relative to their administration. The sacraments, including the Eucharist, were imposed on the people in the main perspective of laws to be observed under pain of mortal sin. The ritualism and legalism that surrounded the whole sacramental life of the Church partially explain why moral theology and the moral instruction of the people were not worked out in the light of the sacraments as a source of life, as celebration and experience of the community of faith, as signs of hope, as a school of vigilance and thanksgiving. The whole presentation of the moral message was severed from the sacrament.

The truth so classically expressed by St. Paul, "You are no longer under law but under the grace of God" (Rom. 6:14), has been fundamentally obscured. The Apostle of the Gentiles teaches the moral message in the context of baptism in such a way that through its celebration, the mystery of Christ and our share in the Paschal Mystery become the law of grace written in our heart. In the legalistic trend of moral theology, precept and control replace the sacrament, which could and should be a dynamic source of joy for our whole life. Thus the Christian who again is "under law" becomes an alienated being, because the law becomes the main perspective. Consequently, sin is reduced to the "transgression of law." The alienation becomes complete when Canon Law and rubrics, even in the less important instances, receive more attention than the law of the holy God himself, which is a law of mercy, of justice, of peace, and of love.

(b) *Alienation through the divorce of morals and dogmatics*

Today, it is again an open question whether the methodological separation between dogmatic and moral theology is a good and workable pragmatism or an alienating dichotomy. However, there can be no doubt that alienation becomes the rule whenever dogmatic theology renounces giving full attention to the dynamics of every salvific truth toward the salvation and wholeness of each man in all his life. There is equally estrangement when a moral teaching neglects to relate its precepts to the values rooted in the truth of salvation: Moral teachings assume true meaning only in a holistic view of the revealed truth.

An immediate consequence of a divorce between dogmatic

and moral theology is a concept of sin against faith where deviation from any abstract formula of faith seems to be a greater sin against faith than an obvious lack of the joy of faith. There is a similar sinfulness in a whole approach to faith that neglects the inborn dynamism of the salvation message toward a life that puts truth into practice. Where this kind of theology speaks of the knowledge of God, or rather, of the knowledge of faith, sins against faith are viewed only or mainly as lack of intellectual knowledge; little attention is given to the want of love, to the lack of adoration that block true progress in the knowledge of the holy God. Once the presentation of dogmatic truth is made sterile, the moral imperatives become unattractive and often repulsive because they are not rooted in that hierarchy of values emanating from a holistic presentation of the truth of salvation. Faith itself is then gradually reduced to an abstract concept of obedience to the Magisterium and to ecclesiastical authorities as representatives of God. So it follows that the whole presentation of the moral message is lacking a noble motivation, namely, the dynamism of faith as the heart of Christian morality.

It often seems that one of the main concerns of St. Paul, "to give morality the right footing in faith" (Rom. 3:30–31), has been thoroughly forgotten or that some tried even to counteract it. Moralism becomes the main enemy of morality since it deprives man of the most effective and salvific motives, namely, the vision and joy of faith. Conscience too seems to be reduced to obedience to the Magisterium and to the ecclesiastical authorities as representatives of God. Very often instead of making room for God, these "representatives" claim to "take the place of God." In such a system of reductionism, neither dogmatic nor moral instruction helps Christians toward maturity.

(c) *Alienation from the love of our neighbor*

With the divorce of morals from the message of faith, the Christian life tends to lose its center, Christ's love imparting and teaching us redeemed and redeeming love toward our neighbor. Thus for some the theological virtue of charity becomes a mere addition to a number of virtues and precepts. Sometimes it is seen as a kind of almsgiving of the wealthy in order to increase their capital for eternal life. In many manuals, love of our neighbor becomes a subdivision of the fifth commandment, and sin against it is conceived basically as damaging one's own perfection. The lion's share is again taken by obedience and a false sacralization of laws. The main approach to moral life followed a self-understanding of the Church that overstressed the institutional aspect. Add to this the alienation involving church structures that arose out of the sacred alliance between throne and altar and since the beginning of the past century because of the restoration with the Church and her concern for political restoration. All this took roots in the very heart of the teaching of morals.

Far be it from us to think of diminishing the value of a mature obedience, the significance of law and order which, indeed, have a sacred value on the condition, however, that they be subordinated to, ordered, and integrated in faith and love of our neighbor. But if they become absolutized and made the central value, then the whole scale of values collapses. Such a chaos is caused by manuals that attach the sanction of eternal condemnation to the smallest rubrics and other church laws of little relevance while matters of love, justice, and peace are easily evaluated as *parvitas materiae* ("small matter"). As a consequence, the absolutized concept of obedience leads to in-fighting, intransigence, intolerance, and seemingly allows the transgression of God's own law of love, mercy, justice, and compassion in favor of minutiae and human traditions.

It seems that many liberals formed in that school continue to exhibit the same mentality in their new stance. They are clamoring for changes and for reforms without any sense for the hierarchy of values. While they are talking about progress and liberation, they neglect and obscure real progress, which comes from faith and love.

(d) *Alienation from the living tradition*

A shocking alienation in morals, particularly with regard to the concept of sin, has been settling down in moral theology because of the superficial sacralization of traditions and of a certain concept of nature and natural law.[11] Consequently, most manuals were not only imprisoned in the past but also hampered a part of the Church from looking confidently ahead and making the most of the present opportunities. Rightly understood, tradition offers a wealth of experience, reflection, and wisdom of past generations, all of which are to be welcomed with great gratitude. But the very sacrilization that leads to ossification deters contemporary man from taking advantage of the past. Sacralized tradition and a static concept of natural law become main obstacles and discourage man in his present search and attempt to integrate the new experiences and reflections with the wisdom of the past. While tradition itself is a stream of life and an appeal to cooperate with the Lord of history, its ossification becomes the great enemy of the future.

In many instances, historical studies have provided evidence that most of the sacralized traditions blocking future perspectives are of relatively recent origin and stand in striking contradiction to the whole of previous traditions. A traditionalism that refuses to free itself becomes an enemy of historical research. The clinging to the status quo and the fixation of the latest tradition contradict and obscure the dynamism of hope and watchfulness for the present opportunities. The cataloguing of sins inspired by such an attitude is a sin against Christ, Redeemer of the whole man and of history.

(e) *The negative influence of an alienated concept of the "states of perfection"*

Those who throughout the centuries followed the evangelical counsels and accepted the Gospel as the rule of their life

11. Bernard Häring, *Morality Is for Persons* (New York: Farrar, Straus & Giroux, 1971).

made a major contribution to prevent and to overcome alienation in the understanding of moral life. But when religious orders and congregations began to identify themselves and their privileges with the "states of perfection" and thus to monopolize sanctity, they became another major cause of alienation in a certain type of moral theology. It is almost inconceivable that all the dynamic commandments of the New Testament could be treated in manuals of moral theology as *opera superogatoria* (which one is tempted to translate as "superfluous works"). The temptation was real for those called to the religious and priestly state to appropriate the whole Christian vocation to sanctity. The alienation of religious and priests that flowed from their many earthly privileges had caused a partial loss of the sense of true sanctity. Expressions such as "self-perfection" and "self-sanctification" revealed a man-centered individualism that also alienated the charism from the community. Since charisms have their meaning only in view of the whole people of God, this spelled a total loss and falsification.

After this appropriation maneuver by the "states of perfection," it remained only for a certain type of moral theology to expropriate or dispossess the lay people by submitting them to a regime of only or mainly limitative laws, since they, as laymen, had not chosen the "states of perfection."

However, I want to emphasize that the great men and women in religious orders and the good priests of the past did not all follow this trend of appropriation and expropriation. I do not treat this question for the sake of generalization but only to explain how a certain kind of moral theology was reduced to a system of laws. Just as today, so also in the past, the difficulties and alienations threatening the priests and religious have been interrelated with the whole process of alienation in the secular world and in the Church. There was a particular reason, however, that sometimes seduced the "states of perfection" to monopolize the vocation to sanctity, namely, their too intimate connection with the privileged classes of society and with that part of a clergy that called itself the "higher clergy."

There is a strong interdependence between renewal of the priestly and religious vocation and renewal of moral theology. The Vatican Council made a particularly important contribution by declaring solemnly, as divinely revealed doctrine, the universal vocation to sanctity. This does not diminish in any way but rather brings rightly to light the vocation of priests and religious. The *Decree on Priestly Formation* affirms that the object of scientific moral theology is "the loftiness of the vocation of the faithful in Christ" (*Optatam Totius*, 16). The consequences for the whole of moral theology and especially for the concept of sin are profound. It becomes evident that an unwillingness to follow the law of grace, the call to continuous conversion, is the great sin blocking the action of the Holy Spirit. An ascetical and moral theology that would still dare to propose "the law of the Spirit" mainly in the perspective of special merit to be acquired through the fulfillment of supererogatory works would be sinning against the very character of grace and charism, indeed against the Holy Spirit who, through the multiplicity of his gifts, calls all together to oneness in Christ.

(f) *Alienation from the environment*

The hiatus between "states of perfection" and the ordinary people "under law only" is one of the reasons why the whole structure of these legalistic manuals could not treat adequately of man's responsibility for his total environment. The highest perfection seemed to be reserved to those who separated themselves from the "world." But unfortunately often they did not think about the godless world of the Gospel of St. John to which no disciple of Christ is allowed to adjust himself, namely the closed, self-righteous world of an arrogant priestly class. Separation from the world was taken to mean separation from the normal conditions of life; it represented practically a negation of man's responsibility to shape the world to the glory of God. But there was more than this one aspect; the whole individualistic and legalistic structure of certain manuals made it impossible to find a constructive approach with respect to responsibility for our environment, which so strongly influences the whole of our life.[12] There was the confluence of many sidestreams into the mainstream of alienation, a kind of original sin. An individualistic concept of the salvation of souls is tied up with a pessimistic vision of the world and the environment; then salvation is seen mainly in the perspective of flight from the proximate occasions of sin. In this atmosphere, it was almost impossible to realize the extraordinary importance of the arduous vocations.[13] A sizable portion of the religious élites alienated themselves from life's environment in order to save their souls. They served the salvation of "souls" only with all the deleterious consequences for themselves and for a milieu suffering from the indifference of the élite.

(g) *Treatises particularly marked by alienation from the community*

The alienations that we have noted thus far were settling into the total structures and perspectives of this kind of moral theology and doctrine on sin. It is impossible to point to all the specific treatises with specific facts, but I can mention a few examples where alienation from solidarity and community is strikingly visible. The treatises of the past century on private property and on justice are among them. The concept of justice was that of the businessman and the establishment, not of the Covenant. It was a protection for the privileged classes which were resisting any new redistribution of earthly goods, and opposing the desire of the expropriates who wanted a share in social responsibilities.

12. See the interesting dissertation of one of my students, G. Biscontin, "Responsibility Toward the Environment: From the Classical Manuals to the Post-conciliar Era" (Rome: Academia Alfonsiana, 1972).

13. See Bernard Häring, *Faith and Morality in the Secular Age* (Garden City, N.Y.: Doubleday, 1973).

Reading some of the treatises on private property, it is hard to avoid the impression that, unconsciously, they were written to favor the pious benefactors of the Church, the powerful and the privileged who gave alms to Church institutions, which so conveniently perpetuated morals that sacralized their privileged status.

There were undoubtedly many other sociological and psychological influences at work, but it cannot be denied that we are faced by a phenomenon of alienation from the spirit of community and universal brotherhood. Only a total conversion and sincere commitment to change the structures of society and of the Church in the direction of solidarity and coresponsibility can allow us to face the social problems of justice and peace in today's world. The very fact that moralists were so much a part of the society and culture of the individualistic Europe of the past should be a wholesome shock for theologians of today. They did promote order and justice within their limited world-view, but they lacked the prophetic spirit characteristic of deep faith.

It would be interesting to study the various causes and forms of alienation in the treatises on chastity and the sins against the sixth commandment among those moralists who were outstanding rigorists and betrayed a real obsession in this matter. However, I again wish to warn against unjust generalizations in the matter of social justice, private property, and the vision of chastity. There were voices in the past as there are today typical of the integrated and well-instructed holy man who manifests his spiritual power in order to overcome alienation and collective prejudices.

(h) *A sinful concept of sin*

Many manuals have a treatise on sin that could well say with the psalmist: "In sin, my mother conceived me." Alienated from the fundamental idea and spirit of the Covenant, the obsession with avoiding sin against law can be translated into a flight from responsibility, a refusal of that coresponsibility that is an exigency of the Covenant. A catalogue of sins in certain manuals often betrays a kind of compensation, a scrupulosity caused by profound alienation from the Covenant. It is, however, rather striking how so many catalogues of sins put out by churchmen came close to the bourgeois ethics. A concept of sin that manifested a great deal of rigorism and intolerance toward others had made the bourgeois self-complacent about itself in its own mediocrity and external correctness.

All this becomes an urgent appeal for conversion and renewal of and by the whole Church community. It can be properly understood only in an awareness of the reality of "original sin," and in relation to the vital decision for salvation in solidarity. The appeal for conversion can be more effective if we realize that the past did produce saints, and among them were moralists and teachers in the Church who maintained a great inner independence and succeeded rather well in overcoming such a sinful concept of sin.

In the next chapter we shall see how the phenomenon of alienation could influence even the concept of original sin. But here when I speak of original sin I am emphasizing the alienation incarnate in the world as a result of all of men's sins and of sinful solidarity. If we are really to understand what sin is and what threats it poses to the whole vision of morality, we have to return to an authentic understanding of faith and of the "law of grace." Once we have found the synthesis in faith, hope, and redeemed love as expression of the covenant with God, sin will be unmasked. "When the law of God is dissected into many commands, the meaning of God's single command to fellowship and to love is no longer understood."[14]

Confronted with the horrifying power of alienation, we should realize that a mere intellectual conversion or a scientific endeavor toward a synthetic vision is not enough. Our

14. G. C. Berkouwer, *Sin* (Grand Rapids, Mich.: Wm. B. Eerdmans, 1971), p. 183.

task can be carried on only in an existential conversion "because that single law (with its various sides and its unique *usus*) can be known only in the context of, and from within, the love of contrition."[15] The very thought that a cold and nonexistential scientific approach could free moral theology from the threat of alienation would be another classical expression of alienation.

6. Sin as Alienation from the History of Salvation and from the Created Universe

A theological approach that is not rooted in the very first article of the creed—the creation of all things in one God—and in the history of salvation will inevitably lead to various forms of alienation. The history of many intellectual movements that were oblivious to or underestimated the reality of the created universe in the light of this one God provides ample evidence to support this thesis. The disincarnate spiritualism that found its most striking expression in gnosticism and in manichaeism is an example. A refusal to consider seriously the first article of the creed led to a specific rejection of the dogma of the Incarnation of the Word of God. But even where spiritualism did not lead to a blunt refusal of the Incarnation, it failed to take it seriously in all its dimensions. Contemplation became flight into the thin atmosphere of ideas, if not into imaginative discussions about the nature of angels and fallen spirits. A false supernaturalization of the salvation of souls overlooked man in his wholeness and in the world.

Lack of interest in and failure to commit oneself to the reality and the vital context of man's life leads to useless speculations about what "would have been" possible. It creates around us a perverted and practically godless world. This is the perspective in which the first letter of St. John sees the disincarnate spiritualism of the gnostics as a godless, alienated world. Where this kind of religiosity prevails, it deprives the

15. Ibid., p. 184.

world around us of the impact of faith because of its refusal to join Christ, the Redeemer of the world.

Today, theology is fully aware that the erroneous concept of original sin as a "stain on the soul" to be washed out by baptism failed to take seriously the impact of sin in the world. This view easily allowed us to refuse responsibility, to turn a deaf ear to our calling to be cooperators of the Redeemer of the world and corevealers of his love to mankind and to the world in which man lives. Theologians could have been speaking about sin and original sin in another way that would have taught man to hear the sighs and travails of the created universe, calling for a share in the liberty of the sons of God (cf. Rom. 8:22).

The intellectual estrangement and theological approaches that alienate man from the created universe and the history of salvation result from the sum total of sins. Each sin rejects the voice of the created universe as it sighs for redemption. A striking example of how alienation in social attitudes can produce a superstructure in theology is found in the theory of limbo. With no foundation in revelation, this theory asserts that all the innocent children who die before being baptized will be deprived of the beatific vision and the communion of saints. They will be exiled to a place of eternal and complete underdevelopment, never to come to a true knowledge of God or to rejoice in his friendship in communion with his friends. They are expelled from the one order of salvation. Such a discourse on the condemnation of innocent human beings to eternal underdevelopment is only possible in the context of a social and religious élite thoroughly unaware of their duty to commit themselves to the development of all men and at all levels. It represents a refusal to give the status of freedom to the great mass of humanity, and leads them to accept the rationalization of such an alienating concept as **limbo.**

Even worse is the doctrine of predestination found in cer-**tain groups** of Calvinists. They teach that God, from the very beginning, in order to manifest his power and majesty, has predestined to beatitude only a small minority while condemning the miserable majority to eternal condemnation. This destroys the whole dynamism of God's commandment of love in brotherhood. It is the kind of seed from which springs the terrible justification of man's inhumanity to man—as colonialism, segregation, discrimination, exploitation, and persecution —which has soiled so many pages of history and is still going on today, and in which so-called Christians participate.

The Afrikaners of the Dutch Reformed Church have up to now justified with the Bible their particularly ugly version of discrimination, apartheid. The basis is that particular predestination doctrine which guarantees to the wealthy and powerful, through their success and parsimony, the certainty of being among the just, the elected, with the right to carry out God's will over the condemned majorities. The situation in South Africa is a strange admixture of old false sacralizations and a new secular pharisaism. Whoever among them have lost interest in religion, or those men who come under the pressures of scientific research, have to acknowledge that the Bible provides no arguments for the segregation and exploitation of the nonwhite population. They therefore resort to all kinds of social and political maneuvers to preserve the present state of affairs, to keep the great majority of the population segregated and fully submissive to the white Afrikaners. The most scandalous aspect comes in that many of these exploiters and sacred liars pray day by day, "lead us not into temptation," while remaining totally unwilling to admit that they themselves have created and are preserving the most colossal institutionalized temptation. They fail to understand that they cannot pray to the one God and Father, pray for liberation from sin unless they are willing to remove the horrifying scandal they have created. They are the cause of many crimes that then come under their hypocritical and vindictive justice.

The very fact that so many forms of sacralization and

alienation have taken roots and become incarnate in religion
itself, particularly in that kind of religion made to serve the
establishment, suggests how difficult renewal and conversion
is, which always remains the first step toward liberty and liberation. Only a total conversion to the living God can open
new vistas leading to a fuller knowledge of him, Creator of all
things and of all men, and of Christ, the Reconciliation, Redeemer, and Lord of the world and of history. Since alienation
bears such a character of totality, a return to God, the Father
and Creator, is sincere and engenders hope only to the extent
that it bears the quality of wholeness.

7. Alienation from the Covenant and from Grace

Wherever the gift of the Covenant and of God's graciousness are minimized, negated, or estranged from the whole of
creation and history, even the virtues, life, and ascetical effort
of those who are just and strong can be tainted by profound
alienation. Whenever asceticism separates human effort from
the source of life, the Lord of the Covenant and his graciousness, one's own justice and justification—whether according
to law or according to any other ethical system—become obstacles to union with God and consequently to the unity of
mankind. And when one's own virtue and energy are not integrated in the perspective of the Covenant and of grace, they
serve as title to self-exaltation. This is one of the main themes
of the theology of St. Paul.

In an individualistic concept of grace and morality, the person lives in view of his own self-sanctification instead of in
view of God's Covenant, and inevitably fails in gratitude
toward God and his people. He does not recognize that all he
has and all that he can do is at the same time a gift of the one
God and Lord and the result of all the good embodied in the
whole people of the Covenant.

Gratitude toward God and toward the community are inseparably bound together. The person who is thankless toward

God, Lord of the Covenant, who gives us his love and thousands of gracious gifts, also forgets and foregoes any gratefulness and responsibility toward the community of salvation. The alienation promoted through individualism and group egotism conceals the insidiousness of an individualistic concept of virtue and sin. Prisoners of this form of alienation will refuse, with an all too good conscience, any generous expression of responsibility and solidarity with others for the good of all; therefore their true identity and the authenticity of Christian freedom will constantly elude them.

8. Sin as Alienation from Oneself and from Others

In an era of secularization it is particularly important to explain the power of sin in terms intelligible to the educated members of our culture. It would be fruitless to present a concept of sin simply as a quality of the soul or in the otherwise important perspective of alienation from God. Sin is also alienation from oneself; it spells disintegration, loss of self-respect, frustration, and disturbance in one's rapport with others. Finally, it threatens self-destruction for the human race itself. Sin is a threat to the wholeness of man. It represents an ever-growing contradiction in one's innermost being. There is no sin against God that does not at the same time affect the whole being of the sinner. It is the embodiment of selfishness and of closed-mindedness.

The disintegration occasioned by sin does not happen all at once; the process of deterioration is gradual. It is not so much the repetition of sin as lack of repentance that erodes the moral freedom and the dynamism of conscience. Impenitence destroys man's innate desire to know and to live truth; he becomes deaf to the appeals of truth and goodness.

The biblical concept *hamartia* indicates this predicament of man's alienation from himself. Man becomes gradually incapable of dwelling within himself and of rejoicing in truth. Distraction and dissipation become enslaving necessities. Vanity, pride, and sensuality become far more enticing than any appeal stemming from the true and the good.

Psychogenic neuroses in general, and more specifically the noogenic neurosis that Viktor Frankl analyzes, represent one way in which the alienation and gradual disintegration of man becomes visible. This phenomenon reflects the cumulative effect of personal sins and of the collective sinfulness incarnate in the world around us. All this is implied in the biblical expression *hamartia*.

Man finds his fulfillment and true self only in his thou-we-I relationships. But as one loses the grace and peace that comes from God, he becomes all the more unable to transcend himself and to establish authentic relationships with others. The sin that damages his capacity to love, to listen, to accept others and to make them happy, destroys man in his inner core. He loses the capacity to be and to become an ever better channel of peace, and so loses his inner harmony. Whoever resists or refuses God's grace can never produce the fruits of the Spirit: "love, joy, peace, endurance, goodness, fidelity, gentleness and self-control" (Gal. 5:22–23).

The alienation reaches down to the whole being of man. It becomes, in the vocabulary of St. Paul, *sarx*, that is, selfishness incarnate. Thus does a man who refuses God's grace condemn himself to that alienation which, of necessity, bears the fruits of selfishness: "fornication, impurity and indecency; idolatry and sorcery; quarrels, a contentious temper, envy, fits of rage, selfish ambitions, dissensions, party intrigues, and jealousies; drinking bouts, orgies and the like" (Gal. 5:19–20).

Sin is not self-destruction of the sinner—if we wish to be accurate in our vocabulary—but it introduces the most jarring contradiction into his personal being. The sinner always remains, in some way, the image and likeness of God, but the more sin takes hold of his existence, the more he becomes a living contradiction of the very name by which God calls him. Hell is not the final destruction of man but that situation where man will remain forever a contradiction to God's calling imprinted in his very nature.

We shall see later how sin diminishes and destroys the fullness of man's freedom, first his freedom as a son of God and then his freedom to desire and do good. Not all sins diminish psychic energies, but every sin diminishes the true freedom—that is, the liberty to rejoice in the good. The more one sins, the more he alienates himself from what is good; goodness is no longer within his reach. Therefore, what should be man's joy is experienced more and more as a strange law imposed from without.

Sin begets sin. Alienation worsens with each unrepented sin. It must therefore be said that the sinner punishes himself. It is in this direction that the theological treatise on punishment for sin must be rethought.[16] We are not allowed to fancy a revengeful God. It is the sinner himself who indulges in self-punishment by alienating himself from God and self, from all the truthfulness and joy of creation. This sin becomes further self-punishment by extending the power of evil. When man has totally expressed himself in his sins, he is condemned. His whole existence becomes punishment: "It would be better for that man if he had never been born" (Mt. 26:24). When sin becomes second nature, then the whole existence of a man is a self-contradiction and spells alienation within his innermost being and in his self-expression.

Man is driven by a dynamic, inborn mechanism to seek his wholeness and integration in love through genuine relationships with God, with his neighbor, and with the world. When these rapports are authentic, then man attains his full identity

16. Karl Rahner, "Punishment of Sins" in *Sacramentum Mundi* VI (1970), pp. 92–94. Good bibliography including C. McAuliffe, "Penance and Reconciliation with the Church" in *Theological Studies* 26 (1965), pp. 1–39. P. Schoonenberg, "Man in Sin" in *Mysterium Salutis* II (1967), p. 864 ff.; by the same author: *Man and Sin: A Theological View* (Notre Dame, Ind.: University of Notre Dame Press, 1965). A. Gélin and Albert Descamps, *Sin in the Bible* (New York: Desclee, 1965). H. E. Brunner, *Man In Revolt: A Christian Anthropology* (London: Lutterworth, 1957). P. Ricoeur, *Fallible Man* (Chicago: Regnery, 1965).

and wholeness. However, sin gradually blocks this integration and frustrates man's attainment of this goal.

9. THE COSMIC AND ENVIRONMENTAL DIMENSION OF SIN

The personal dimension of frustration is by no means the only one. Sin also pervades man's environment and thereby assumes a truly cosmic dimension. A man who disregards the grace and charisms of God is not only refusing his own freedom and dignity but deprives and fails the whole of creation, which expects from him the manifestation of the freedom of the sons and daughters of God. Because of its intimate solidarity with mankind, the whole created universe suffers and sighs under the frustration produced by the totality of sins. Man receives God's grace in order to act as mediator of salvation. His mission extends to the created universe, that it may be freed more and more from the slavery of corruption and frustration (Rom. 8:20–24).

The person who refuses to grow in the knowledge of God makes himself accountable for the increasing density of darkness in the world, although by his God-given nature and by grace he is called to be light for the world, a candle to enkindle the light in many others. God's work is intended to come to fulfillment in a saving solidarity among men. Sinful mankind tends instead to involve the whole created world and all the gifts of God, destined for all, in a consolidation of perdition.

Man is the free first cause of sin. There cannot be a discourse on sin in its true sense whenever or wherever man has no choice other than to do evil. It is precisely because he can choose solidarity in salvation that his choice of solidarity in sin is so horrifying. Where man prefers alienation, he cannot escape being enslaved in the corruption and frustration of the world, a frustration that he himself increases. "Sin is nothing and has nothing and can do nothing apart from the beings and powers which God has created. Yet it organizes all these for rebellion against him."[17] The truth that sin always involves the world created by God, and seeks to organize the good energies for solidarity in evil, is one of the most profound and most shocking reasons for total conversion to a constructive coresponsibility for the world in which we live.

The collective sinfulness of the Pharisees who rejected Christ stands as a most striking example of the density of frustration and alienation that corrupts the total environment. Their systematic abuse of religion for self-enhancement created a corrupt establishment. People associated with it could no longer breathe truth nor rejoice in it. "Alas for you, lawyers and Pharisees, hypocrites! You travel over sea and land to win one convert; and when you have won him you make him twice as fit for hell as you are yourselves. Alas for you, blind guides" (Mt. 23:15–16).

The closed and practically godless world that resulted from the dynamism of the combined sins of the Pharisees and scribes can be a tremendous obstacle to the true knowledge of God. "Alas for you lawyers! You have taken away the key of knowledge. You did not go in yourselves, and those who were on their way in, you stopped" (Lk. 11:52). Their bad example, their words, and the very structures tainted by their sins were the means by which the Pharisees and priests seduced the people. Through them, all became involved in the refusal of Christ. This event probably represents the apogee of collective responsibility and incarnate alienation, the "sin of the world."

For many theologians today—Schoonenberg, for instance—this sin seems to be a more decisive event in the history of the world's sin than that committed by the first sinful man. This is symbolically expressed by the earthquake at the time of Christ's crucifixion. A refusal of God's own Son by a sinful world rocks the whole of creation. This event is an omnipresent feature of the history of Israel—indeed, of the whole

17. Berkouwer, op. cit., p. 65. He is quoting H. Balinck, *Gereformeerde Dogmatiek* III, 126.

of mankind. If the Jews had accepted Christ, they would not have run into violence and wars against the Romans; Jerusalem would not have been destroyed. But this is only a secondary aspect of the whole reality. The destruction of Jerusalem, the dispersion of the Jews, and the subsequent pitiful anti-Semitism are a few of the manifestations of alienation that settled down in the whole history of man and the universe.

Collective alienation as a consequence of all the sins of mankind becomes a terrifying historical phenomenon. Instances are many: the hunting and torturing of witches, which was sanctioned even by the Church; all forms of collective intolerance and fanaticism found in colonialism; the superiority complex of some races, especially of the European and North American cultures; the massacre of the Indians of North and South America; neocolonialism and ethical colonialism, where one culture seeks to impose its norms on others as absolutely binding; a totally profit-oriented economy; the myth of consumerism with the artificial creation of needs and wants that in no way serve the human person; the refusal to cooperate in a better distribution of earthly goods and capacities; we could go on *ad infinitum*. Take only the example of racism in Australia, which keeps out virtually all oriental immigrants; the responsible men of Australia thus become partially accountable for the millions of abortions plaguing Japan in the past decades. It is above all the collective prejudices, a poisoned public opinion that is a greater evil than air and water pollution. This should suffice to convey the idea of the alienating power of sin.

Man is an intellectual being. If he is born and lives in an environment where lying is, as it were, institutionalized, he cannot come to the light unless he joins all those who are able and willing to create an enlightened environment where truthfulness shines through. I allude again to the appalling example of the Republic of South Africa. A child of Afrikaners who are members of the Dutch Reformed Church not only shares in their overprivileged situation relative to earthly goods but also in their partial or total blindness with respect to the dignity of men of other races and churches. The sin of racism is a collective sin that allows so many calloused consciences to pursue the most outrageous form of segregation of blacks, Asians, and other nonwhites. If anyone adjusts to such a subhuman type of society and culture, he can no longer respect himself as a person. Since the Afrikaner is unable to respect and appreciate men of other cultures or races as persons, he cannot practically recognize his own dignity as a person, even though he exalts himself as a member of a superior but exploiting class. In such an environment, where one is cut off from the common endeavor of men of good will, a member of the Dutch Reformed Church transforms what he calls praise and prayer into a "sacred lie." How can a man call God "Creator and Father of all men" or "Our Father" when he so blatantly rejects the brotherhood, the equality of persons of other races?

Once we have understood the dreadful power of alienation embodied in institutional structures and in public opinion, it becomes all the more evident that a one-sided ethic of obedience that produces uniformity and enslavement under collective prejudices is no more than another form of alienation and of complicity in the sin of the world. The same applies to an ethics that preaches only sentiment, interior feelings, or vague attitudes while failing to lead or to educate toward courageous responsibility and prophetic frankness.

10. SIN AS DECAY

Every sin is simultaneously a manifestation and a promotion of decay. Whoever indulges in evil that could be avoided or omits the good expected of him gradually loses the dynamism toward healthy freedom and responsibility. Decay in the Church as well as decay in whole cultures or decay of good customs is brought about by numerous sins and invites to more sin.

Sin is often revealed in indolence or inertia, in static repetition and restoration, with all the implications of self-deception and of deception of others insofar as it is presented under the guise of fidelity. This kind of refusal of loyalty to the God of history becomes enslavement to the past. It deserves, as patron and guide, the wife of Lot who, looking backward, was immobilized. Constant lamentation about our "bad times" and flight into pessimism and wishful thinking—"if only I were living in another world"—are manifestations of immobilism, of spiritual laziness and lack of vigilance for today's opportunities. The sinner and the sinful world refuse the offer of the present hour and choose alienation by living in a world that is past while lamenting the present.

Sin is not only disobedience to existing norms but is often expressed in a refusal to look for and work out new norms in view of true progress and authentic conversion. Sin is always an enemy of the sense and finalism of history, an obstacle to the development of freedom. Whether individual or collective, sin is always in opposition to the history of salvation.[18]

This flight into the past, which destroys the dynamism of the living tradition, is truly sin because Christ is not only the point Omega of the whole history before him, but also the gracious offer of the present hour and of the hope and dynamism toward the future. Redemption is openness to the history of the future, the expectation of the coming of Christ in the events of history, and thus is vigilance for the real opportunities of the here and now.

The worldview of evolution and history is classically formulated in the thought of Teilhard de Chardin. The decisive moments are the creative leaps that prepare hominization and are dynamically directed toward the coming of Christ. When sin does not intercept the dynamism of history, a growing consciousness of God's presence results, a deeper knowledge of God and a more appealing realization of brotherhood in

18. P. Schoonenberg, "Man in Sin" in *Mysterium Salutis* II (1967), p. 851.

God. A static approach, on the contrary, rooted in the attitude of restoration of the past, pits itself against the development of history and mankind. Implicitly, this longing for bygone days discloses refusal of the Lord of history.

The philosophy of history of the past century, which so greatly influenced liberalism and Marxism, states that the progress of history does not await man's free decision on the moral and religious level. Dialectic materialism believed in the automatic power of the dialectic, growing hatred and struggle of classes which, after increasing the misery of the poor, would lead to the salvific explosion of liberation. Because of this ideology, classical Marxism opposed all realistic reforms and so became a striking expression of alienation and decay. It failed to see that liberation must be freely invested in the present hour. Karl Marx could not imagine the renewing power of nonviolent action, and freedom as fruit of redemption. Since he rejected faith in the God of love, his whole system became flight from Him and an alienation from the true sense of history. At the same time, it incited and invited new modes of alienation and decay.

11. Sin as Alienation from Truth

Holy Scripture describes sin as darkness (*skotos*), as lie and mendacity (*pseudos*), as self-deception and deceitfulness with others, and as a consequence, the whole situation is illusory and alienating from truth (*apate*). A man who does not act according to what he knows to be true and habitually refuses to put truth into practice is deceiving himself while philosophizing about truth. A sinner who does not repent transforms himself all the more into a liar. In the end, the hopeless sinner is "one who loves and practises deceit" (Rev. 21:8 and 22:15). Sin gradually estranges man from God, who is at once truth and love, and enslaves man in an ever firmer net of error and deceit (Rom. 1:24 ff. and 3:4).

This situation of mendacity and deceit is not only a reality in the mind and heart of the sinner; his self-deception is inter-related with the darkness and deceit of "the liar's kingdom." It is an expression of solidarity in reasons and motives so construed as to reject Christ and avoid the demands of a knowledge of God. All is happening within the realm of darkness, which overtakes those who alienate themselves from God's saving truth (Jn. 12:35). Inevitably man falls under the tyranny of mendacity, manipulation, and deceit unless he decides to live within the community of faith, to unite himself with all men of good will in a sincere search for what is true and good (*GS*, 16).

Where the slavery of mendacity and deceit grips man, the air is filled with empty talk of liberty, independence, self-determination, growth, and humanity. All too often, sinful man wants to be considered modern, a man without any preju-dices, enlightened and liberal. "Men prefer darkness to light because their deeds are evil. Bad men all hate the light and avoid it, for fear their practices should be shown up" (Jn. 3:19–20). This implies that the sinner not only tries to hide what he is doing but that he covers it by proclaiming it zeal for justice, an effort at updating, or some other noble cause. "Satan himself masquerades as an angel of light. It is there-fore a simple thing for his agents to masquerade as agents of good" (II Cor. 11:14–15). The climax of deceit is reached in the pious talk of the priests and Pharisees who refuse Christ and call him a partner of Beelzebub (Mk. 3:22).

A similar process is going on among those who constantly defame the Church as a conservatory of men craving power and deceit. I am not referring here to those who criticize the Church because of their belief in it as a pillar of truth: Such constructive critics are working hard for the renewal of the Church.

Each new sin that finds no remedy in sorrow and con-version becomes a further impediment to light and to the true knowledge of God. "The essence of sin is to lay roadblocks to all true knowledge of our sin. . . . Our knowledge of sin is constantly thwarted by sin's own deception and sham, and its own manner of presenting itself to us and tempting us."[19]

Moral theology today is freeing itself from that one-sided consideration of the isolated individual act of decision that so often allows man to excuse himself on the basis of ignorance or lack of deliberation. Rather, we look to a dynamic process in terms of whether one is en route to a fuller union with truth or whether one is plunging into greater darkness. We can no longer ignore the trickery of an environment that is alienated from God's truth. In many instances, however, the distraction, the basic lack of awareness and sensitivity of a person who, while doing wrong, does not think through the sinfulness of his decision in the light of the gospel, this very process of decay can well be the product of a long process of self-deception and alienation from truth. Instead of absolving himself by "I didn't know it," he had better pray, "Lord, have mercy on me; I am a sinner!"

The person who conceals the real situation from himself, and the social group that seeks to justify its injustice, are often extremely severe in their judgment of others. They will not come to their senses without a prophetic shock; they need a kind of electroshock therapy if they are to break out of their subtle game of self-deception. The prophet Nathan fulfilled this role with David when he had stolen the wife of Uriah and had killed him. "One day a traveller came to the rich man's house and he, too mean to take something from his own flocks and herds to serve his guest, took the poor man's lamb and served up that. David was very angry and burst out: 'As the Lord lives, the man who did this deserves to die! He shall pay for the lamb four times over, because he has done this and shown no pity.' Then Nathan said to David, 'You are the man'" (II Sam. 12:4–7).

The alienating power of sin finds particular corroboration in today's life in the manipulation of public opinion and in the mendacity and hypocrisy with which overprivileged and pow-

19. Berkouwer, op. cit., p. 150.

erful classes justify social structures and political maneuvers. An analysis of the Marxist language shows countless examples. It suffices to remember the pious talk of "brotherly help" when Dubcek's reform socialism was routed out by Soviet and allied tanks. Capitalism, too, can claim no exemption from this fog of self-deception.

Alienation from truth becomes particularly lamentable where dry orthodoxy attempts to hide, behind a diplomacy of reformism, its unreadiness to be converted and to commit itself to a real reform. Alienation is complete when the desire to make an ecclesiastical career determines everything, even to the point of using religion for self-aggrandizement and for domination over others.

This horrifying image of alienation from truth underlines again the importance of a community of faith and adoration, of a common effort to live that sincerity so central to the Sermon on the Mount. It all pleads for a humble confession of our sins, for fraternal correction, and for a communitarian revision of life. The humble confession to a brother in Christ can dissipate many shades of untruthfulness; but the individual confession alone, made in the dark confessional box on a totally anonymous basis, cannot break the fetters of alienation. Confession has to fight against the total power of darkness, and therefore the individual confession calls also for a communitarian revision of life and for the prophetic witness that helps a community become more and more a light for the world.[20]

12. PHARISEES IN THE CHURCH AND IN THE SECULAR WORLD

The prototype of alienation from the truth is the Pharisee. For the sake of justice, however, it must be said that not all members of their sect can be identified with the biblical judgment on "pharisaical" attitudes and groups. The embodiment

20. See Bernard Häring, *Christian Renewal in a Changing World* (Garden City, N.Y.: Doubleday, 1968), pp. 287–99.

of pharisaism reaches its peak in those persons and groups which, because of their sacred egotism and their alienation from true religion, have rejected Christ. They represent a type that is constantly recurring in the history of the Church and of the world. The point here is that alongside the clerical Pharisee one can find the typical Pharisee of the secular world. The Pharisee is everywhere present, not only in "the establishment" but also within groups of "reformers," protesters, and terrorists.

(a) *The clerical Pharisee*

This person seeks his security in religion understood as a system of laws, in a sterile cult and in a well-defined system of orthodoxy. He abuses religion for the sake of safeguarding his class privileges, and judges others by his own rules and norms. He binds heavy burdens and places them on men's shoulders but does not raise a finger to lift the load himself (Mt. 23:4). He ostensibly works for God's glory while in reality all is done for display. His whole behavior thus reveals a striking alienation from the living God. His moralism is evasion. His sharp judgments arise from his self-righteousness and his unreadiness to be converted to the living God and to the great commandment of love, mercy, and justice.

The clerical Pharisee insists on the most insignificant precepts, which he scrupulously observes. It is a compensatory scrupulosity; for instance, he violently condemns whoever allows himself a minimum of spontaneity and creativity in the liturgy because such behavior disturbs his security complex. He judges such persons as transgressing a law which, to him, means power of control and external security. On the fundamental questions of morality and adoration of God, the Pharisee is extremely lax with himself but most severe on others. "You strain off a midge, yet gulp down a camel!" (Mt. 23:24). All this is a play of self-defense calculated to avert the call to self-conversion. The ritual scrupulosity helps him conceal from himself the fact that inside he is "filled with robbery and self-indulgence" (Mt. 23:25).

The clerical Pharisee condemns most severely the secular world. He is particularly apt in lamentations and harsh judgments about fashion and lax customs but has little sensitivity about problems of social justice and peace. He despises the world outside, those who do not belong to his caste or to the Church as he conceives her to be. It is surprising that the clerical Pharisee has never been able to understand that it is precisely this kind of man, who has set up an artificial religious world and who alienates himself from the hopes, joys, and anxieties of mankind, whom Christ calls a hopeless and alienated "world." It is also amazing how outrageously certain groups of traditionalists in the clergy and laity fight over minutiae, unreal problems, while remaining totally blind to the great opportunities and the needs of mankind today.

(b) *The Pharisee of the secularist world*

The secularist Pharisee is by no means inferior to his clerical counterpart; indeed, he is likely to feel morally superior to him since he has finally and totally broken with religion. He shares the clerical Pharisee's lack of true knowledge of God. By his decision to ignore God, he defends himself against the call to conversion arising from within and from without. He avoids all sincere and humble search for the ultimate value of life, and finally justifies his own moral and religious situation by an increasing rigorism and harshness in his judgments of Church institutions, all religions and individual believers. Within the secular community, this kind of Pharisee is not less intolerant and prone to judge others than the cleric within his religious caste and sect.

(c) *The Pharisee of the establishment*

Not only the Pharisee who sits on Moses' chair but also those of the secular establishment preach to their subjects strict observance of the law and obedience. They want conversion to their bourgeois morality. On this point, the clerical

Pharisee and the Pharisee of the secular establishment have much in common. Both are blind to the signs of the times; both have their eyes fastened on morals and law, if not religion, as a means of defending their own security and that of their inflexible institutions. They hide their stubborn opposition to necessary reforms by busying themselves in a vague reformism, and use a thousand and one moral arguments to conceal the real motive, their hunger and thirst for power and for preservation of their privileges. Since they absolutize their inherited situation, they speak with moral indignation against all those who seek real reform.

An amusing example of the affinity between clerical Pharisaism and a certain kind of traditional bourgeois mentality is the Italian magazine *Il Borghese* ("the bourgeois"), an expensive, luxurious, pornographic right-wing periodical that for years has extended gracious hospitality to the clerical traditionalists. Both join forces in fighting communism, and of course everyone is Communist who does not share their concern for the establishment and their capitalistic tendencies. Both the clerical and the secular Pharisees are in favor of a most rigorous vindictive justice toward anyone who transgresses their law and does not abide by their bourgeois morality. They need this zeal for the law in order to justify to themselves their unwillingness to reform institutions and structures that have become institutionalized temptations for so many. They are unwilling and unable to see that their own attitude is the basic cause of extremism, frontal protests, and a good deal of today's criminality. While blind to their own violence and the violence of the structures and methods that protect the egotism of their own privileged classes, they accuse even the most innocuous nonviolent protest of delusion and intolerance.

(d) *The Pharisee of protest and violent subversion*

We should not be blind to the Pharisaism of many of those who call for renewal and who preach a total revolution against all alienating structures. Many of the "professional protesters" who are loudly condemning all institutions and everyone within them, even those who honestly try to serve mankind, embody in a particularly obnoxious way the qualities of the Pharisee. They have all the tendencies to overgeneralization and to the censorious attitudes of the old Pharisees. Like them, they refuse to examine their own consciences. The restless pharisee of this kind has no constructive ideas; he is totally taken up with his overreaction to institutions. The louder he calls for "love," the more he spreads hatred; the louder he shouts for justice, the less willing he is to do justice to those whom he opposes. In relation to those who bear the burden of office and are engaged in a patient struggle for renewal, he is as blind as the biblical Pharisee who was unable and unwilling to recognize a truly prophetic voice. History provides ample evidence about violent revolution: The revolutionary who becomes enthroned all too often becomes a more violent oppressor than the one against whom he incited the bloody revolution. He usually becomes intransigent and fanatically rigid in his judgments of those who favor change.

In keeping with one of the main perspectives of this book, I should like to make here a point which should not be forgotten. If this sort of discussion of Pharisaism in the Church and in the secular world were to serve primarily our own self-defense and self-justification, we ourselves would be incorrigible pharisees. If, after their sad experiences with Hitler, harassed people all over the world had the courage to search for the Hitler in themselves, so must Christians have the courage to look for the hidden atheist and pharisee in themselves. Only if together we strive toward personal conversion and renewal of structures and institutions can we suppress the trend toward pharisaism. Only together can we return to truth and truthfulness and find that balance that does justice to institutions and to a passionate desire for renewal.

13. Idols and Ideologies in an Alienated World

Collective and individual alienation from truth, and all kinds of pharisaism find embodiment in idols and ideologies. Marxism asserts that everything the Church stands for and teaches is nothing but an ideology.[21] Marx believed that religion is only a superstructure of an alienated economy, which makes diplomatic use of ideas in favor of the establishment and privileged upper class. This is an unjust and blind generalization.

In no way is divine Revelation an ideology. On the contrary, it liberates man from his ideologies and his idols. Everyone who has had a genuine religious experience can attest to the fact that a religious truth that we accept in faith is a truth that humbles us and calls for self-denial and liberation from any desire to enjoy special privileges or to dominate over others. Revelation is a saving and liberating truth. It calls man to be a servant with Christ the Servant. It is striking, for instance, that the gospel clearly speaks of the sins and of the partial alienation of the apostles, especially Peter. If the gospels were an ideology in the service of a power-oriented Church, it would be unthinkable for them to unmask the alienating attitudes of the disciples of Christ. Furthermore, the gospels use the strongest words and examples to condemn the false expectations of a power Messiah and national hero. Scripture does likewise for those believers who would make the charisms of their vocation an argument for superiority and power-seeking. We know from the history of salvation that original sin creates all kinds of temptation to abuse even religious truths and institutions for one's own vanity, but it is lack of real faith that causes anyone to submit to that temptation. Our religion requires us to submit ourselves to the judgment of truth so that Christ's truth can make us free.

21. Cf. W. Post, "Ideology" in *Sacramentum Mundi* III (New York: 1969), pp. 94–97, with bibliography.

An ideology is almost the same, on a collective level, as the diplomatic use of truth by an individual person. For instance, a man who thinks first of the impact of his actions and words on his hoped-for career is looking only indirectly at the meaning of truth itself. This phenomenon is all too common in the secular world and unfortunately occurs also in the Church.

Renewal of the Church and of society demands an ongoing critique of ideologies, that is, discernment in terms of a humble serving and acceptance of truth. There should be no lessening of effort even where it humbles us and calls us to a change and conversion from that kind of alienation in the field of knowledge that results from power structures and selfish persons and groups wanting to dominate or exploit others for personal gains.

One of today's most discussed questions in Catholic theology may illustrate this point. I refer to the matter of infallibility of the Church and specifically of Peter's successor. My own firm conviction is that the dogma of the infallibility of the Church and of Peter is not an ideology. In itself, it is a liberating truth. But in practice it is possible to misinterpret it and transform it partially into an ideology, and this sinful approach to the charisma promised to the Church, not the dogma itself, is extremely dangerous. It suffices to study the historical circumstances to see that this dogma, from the very beginning of the First Vatican Council, was threatened by ideological tendencies. The most intransigent members of the Curia and participants in the Council itself were not at all satisfied with its result, since the definition of infallibility literally meant "limitation," a clear-cut indication of the limits within which we can speak of papal infallibility.

Immediately after the First Vatican Council, the same group of persons for whom spiritual power, wrongly understood, meant compensation for the loss of the temporal power of the Church, initiated a process of amplifying the doctrine of papal infallibility to the point that they demanded a "sub-

mission of faith" to almost everything issuing from the Pope
or the Holy Office. Typical in this respect is the vocabulary
of certain theologians who, even today, assert that some doctrines, even though they are not dogmas, are to be considered
as absolutely irreformable. In other words, even where there
can be found no guarantee of divine Revelation and no certainty of the absolute assistance of the Holy Spirit to protect
from error, they remain totally unwilling to progress in the
knowledge of truth and to correct partial errors.

Although we have begun to exemplify the critique of ideologies with examples from the ecclesial environment, we
must never forget that the secular world often is the natural
habitat of ideology. I must therefore address myself to this
point now.

An ideology, insofar as it means an arbitrary and often arrogant approach to "truths" and the manipulation of communication, comes very close to the concept of idol. A man who
does not adore the true and living God with all his heart and
with his whole life is necessarily yielding to some idols. He
then becomes a coworker in the fabrication of ideologies.

While the Christian vision of history and eschatology believes in the dynamism of history because of the presence of
the Lord of history with his healing and reconciling power,
the *faith of many secularists in a constant and necessary progress of history* becomes an ideology. This kind of philosophy
of history has had great impact on European thought since
the middle of the past century. Man, who made himself independent of faith and revelation, kept God out of history and
convinced himself that the progress of culture and of humanism is automatic and necessary. Marxism adapted this ideology in its own way to justify class hatred and the resultant
class struggle. Because of this ideology, Marxists refused any
effort toward patient and gradual renewal. Their ideology
impelled them to arouse hatred and strife in the hope that this
dialectic would bring the saving explosion of the revolution of
the proletariat.

Stalinism and other forms of "orthodox Marxism" are striking models of ideology and the manipulation of communication in the hands of those who consider themselves accredited heirs and administrators of the Marxist truths. They teach and impose their doctrine violently while, consciously or not, orienting it always to serve their privileged bureaucratic role. Think only of the terminology used to justify the invasion of Czechoslovakia in 1968. Oppression of a nation was declared "fraternal help." The Marxist restoration in Prague was proclaimed as a great step forward.

Another dangerous idol that produces numerous ideologies is the pride and spiritual sloth of the *homo faber*, the technical man. It found a classical expression in the capitalist liberalism of Adam Smith, David Ricardo, and the like; their ideology insisted on the autonomy of the economy and refused all interference from morality and religion in the field of economics. Of course, a moralism that would impose its laws without adequate knowledge of the functioning of economic life must be equally opposed.

In the case of the ideology of Adam Smith and his school, their interest in the economic success and the perpetuation of the privileges of an upper socio-economic class was such that it refused integration with a more spiritual outlook and the inclusion of trade justice in the social justice of mankind.

Although Marxism came as a violent reaction against liberalism and capitalism, it nevertheless inherited the same idol and therefore produced similar ideologies. One of them is the thesis that the economic life is the infrastructure that fundamentally decides all other social structures of life. In capitalism, as in Marxism, this basic ideology of the *homo faber* serves as justification for all types of manipulation, and is part and parcel of the effort—mostly unconscious—to construct a too good conscience about his hidden incapacity or unreadiness to open himself to spiritual values and to commit himself unselfishly without economic or material rewards.

I maintain that we of the Western world have every reason

not to condemn too loudly Marxism or its ideologies without equally unmasking the pharisaism and ideology of *Western materialism*. Many of the harsh attacks leveled at communism are defense mechanisms of the *homo faber* of the West who is not ready to open himself to a profound reform of his thinking and of the structures of his life.

I have already spoken of the idol and ideology of *racism*, which has found its greatest explosion in Hitler's national socialism, but we can speak of this ideology only by soul-searching, by examining ourselves about the hidden "Hitler in us." The idol remains, even with a religious twist, in the racism of South Africa and other parts of the world. Only a collective alienation from truth and from a serious search for higher values can explain such an enormous chaos of values behind which whole groups, classes, and nations defend themselves. Their social injustice is coupled with an unreadiness to commit themselves to a real reform in all-embracing fraternity, in efforts to help the traditionally exploited to take their own part, share, and responsibility in the common development.

Another striking ideology is that of the pragmatic *utilitarianism* of so many persons who bring philanthropic concerns to the fore precisely where they are promoting most inhumane approaches. It suffices to mention the world-wide crusade not only to remove legal sanctions against abortion but to promote abortion, one of the most lucrative new enterprises. In the state of New York alone, half a million legalized abortions were recorded in the first two years following the passage of the abortion law. Since June 1, 1970, there has been a mushrooming of abortion clinics and abortion agencies which, for good fees, assure maximum service to the existing abortion clinics and to the opening of new facilities as the demand grows. In this polluted atmosphere a gynecologist informs his colleagues that he has come upon his gold mine. This capitalistic ideology wields such power over the mass media of communications as to make it instrumental in manipulating public opinion and politics.

Sex consumerism in the post-Puritan era constitutes another fertile ground of ideologies. More than at any past historical moment sexuality has become a commodity in the great public market. The ideology manifests itself in a pseudopsychology, pseudosociology, in the service of the whole system of publicity and other structures intent on exploiting sexual appetites and disorders while seeking to justify such exploitation. The new idols of the playboy and sexy girl are becoming part of the daily publicity fare. *Playboy* seeks to gain respectability for its pornographic pages through articles by and about famous men and women. Another already mentioned tragic example is the Italian pornographic magazine *Il Borghese*, which presents itself as protector of the stable order; in spite of its traditional anticlericalism, it reports interviews with monsignors and supermonsignors. A stupendous output of books and reports from study commissions glorify pornography and pornofilms as signs of the liberation of mankind. In reality it is one of the most enslaving phenomena of our times, and a typical example of the manipulation imposed on many by a permissive society.

In certain circles, either *conservatism* or *liberalism* are idols fabricating their respective ideologies. There are environments in which an accusation of conservatism is equivalent to a death sentence. One has to be progressive and liberal at all cost; there is little concern for truth and human balance. In this way talk about renewal and a better world can also become an idol; it has in fact produced numerous forms of ideology. So has traditionalism. Tradition becomes an absolute behind which hide spiritual laziness and a security complex; traditionalists too wear masks of philosophy, and sometimes of experimental psychology and sociology.

Modern critique of ideologies was introduced by Francis Bacon (1561–1626) and spread especially through the *Novum*

Organum. According to Bacon, the idols and collective prejudices have roots in basic idols (1) *idola tribus*, the idols of the tribe, that is, all ideologies caused by the frailty of human nature as such and reinforced by the misery of a closed tribal society (I should like to add: all this flows from collective sin and from individual sins in the past, a reality which in theological terms is called "the sin of the world" and/or "the original sin"); (2) *idola specus*, the idols of the cave, caused by the limitations of the human intellect of men that plunges into all kinds of darkness because of their own particular constitution, education and habits, the accidental circumstances, and the past sins; (3) *idola fori*, the idols of the market place which derive from society and language (today we are reminded of the ideologies that invest in the mass media of communication, in the very language, for instance, of the bankrupt Third Reich of Hitler—numerous studies have been conducted on the impact of nazism on the whole language); (4) *idola theatri*, the idols of the theater that include all preconceived syllogisms and erroneous assertions of philosophy and tradition; such idols are set up with theatrical styles of life where so many people play roles not in keeping with their personal identity. These are found in the lives of individuals and groups who think more of the impression they make on others, of social prestige and economic success, than of a sincere search for existential truth. The academic world is not always exempt from this kind of idols.

Today, critique of ideology is a very important approach in the scientific world and can be extremely useful for the Church and for the secular world. It is indispensable in philosophy, theology, and in the behavioral sciences whenever they want to make themselves normative sciences, transgressing their limits. Behind all idols and ideologies, there stands the sin of the alienation of the individual men and of whole collectivities who do not long for the knowledge of God; "these are people who have no sense of truth" (Is. 1:3). The effective exposure of idols and ideologies becomes possible only in the context of individual conversion and social renewal. For people who refuse self-criticism and the need for conversion, even the most elaborate scientific approach to a critique of ideology will be pharisaism.

Our reflection results also in a clear intuition that the individual confession, important as it is, needs integration into a communitarian revision of life. The celebration of the sacrament of penance must be integrated more and more into the task of reconciliation in all its personal and social aspects. The Church cannot be, nor can it celebrate, the sacrament of reconciliation without listening to the prophetic voices; and indeed the prophets and their voices are sometimes quite discomforting. Whenever Israel fell into the slavery of ideologies and worshiped idols, God in his mercy sent prophets; but often the kings and the priests, as well as the people seduced by them, did not receive the prophets.

14. Genuine Anthropocentric Humanism and Alienated Humanism

The humanism of the Renaissance, and even more the humanism of today's secularism, remain still chained to a great extent to the reaction against religion's discarnate theocentrism and institutional verticalism. Hence they are as alienated and alienating as the extreme against which they are reacting, or perhaps more so, since they apparently remain unaware that while the religious presentation has greatly changed, they have not. In this situation, we have to investigate the diverse forms and causes of secular anthropocentrism and the various admixtures that taint contemporary humanism, in order to understand better the genuine expression of theological anthropocentrism.

In the ethical prophetism of Israel there is already a marvelous synthesis of theocentrism, with a passionate interest in man as such. Jesus Christ, true God and true man, is the absolute climax of the theocentric and anthropocentric vision. He who "descended from heaven for us men and for our salvation" makes the Father's glory visible by giving himself totally to the service of all men. The theocentric and anthropocentric, if rightly understood, are two aspects of one and the same approach, which focuses on the synthesis of the two commandments: to love God with all our energies and to love our neighbor and ourselves in an authentic and redeemed love.[22]

While it cannot be denied that the salvation of the whole man has always been an important theme of theology and of the preaching of the Church, it must be equally acknowledged that it did not always characterize the basic approach of theological thought. Above all, the concept of salvation was often alienated and all too narrow, due to an extreme verticalism and a one-sided emphasis on the "soul" instead of on the salvation and liberation of the whole human person in the total context of human history and in all of man's interaction with the world. Thus the very theme of the salvation of souls became, in part at least, an alienation.[23]

The influence of diverse philosophies, especially that of the Greeks and the Persian philosophy of Zoroaster, of gnosticism and Manichaeism have led, even in orthodox circles, to a theology where the salvation of the whole man was not always the central theme of God's self-revelation.

If we scrutinize the thoroughness with which some theologians of past centuries dealt with the psychology of the angels and the principle of their individuation, there is reason for hilarity but also for sadness, since there was no bond whatsoever with man's history of salvation. A certain dogmatic theology boasted of its own scientific character when

22. Joseph Splett, "Humanism and Anthropocentrism" in *Sacramentum Mundi* III (1969), pp. 78–79.

23. See Chapter 4, where the full concept of salvation and liberation will be treated in greater detail.

it studied God "in himself," beyond revelation, and outside the context of his love for man. Thus it severed the discourse on God from the treatise on man.

Another example of the same frame of mind is a theology that was probing all facets of the validity and licitness of sacraments but never dreamed that man, as the image and likeness of God, should, in Jesus Christ, become the main sacrament of God's saving presence, and that consequently this calling should be central to any discourse on the sacraments. This is not possible without concentrating on the knowledge of man. However, very often manuals of moral theology, as well as of dogmatic theology, were clinically "clean" of any anthropology. Some would speak on natural law without exerting any specific effort to understand man in his wholeness and in his various historical contexts. They took as starting point an abstract concept of being (*ens*) or the generic nature of animals and thus came to the conclusion that "natural law is what nature teaches all animals."[24]

It cannot be denied that in many manuals of theological schools a number of dogmas were treated without any clear reference to the work of the redemption and liberation of man. It was not made clear that God revealed himself by revealing his redeeming and liberating love to mankind. All too often, theologians overlooked the fact that according to the Scriptures, God has entrusted man himself and the whole world to the responsible use of man's freedom. Theological treatises often left the impression that God could be looked upon as a stopgap who would fill the holes within the fabric of man's utilities.

Fully aware that today's atheism and secularism are forms of radical reaction against a disincarnate theocentrism, a number of the most influential theologians have worked out a systematic critique of all theology in a perspective of an-

24. Thomas Aquinas, *Summa Theologica* I–II ae, 9, 94, a 2. This article of the *Summa* is referred to in *Humanae Vitae*, footnote 9 to Article 10, where the biological laws seem to be given the main relevance in the definition of "natural law."

thropocentric renewal which, however, would by no means contradict or weaken true theocentrism.[25] This anthropocentric theology focuses chiefly on eliminating, as completely as possible, all philosophical, political, juridical, ritualistic, and theological alienation in theology and in the practices of the Church, trying to achieve instead an authentic synthesis between the glory of God and the salvation of mankind, between biblical theocentricism and biblical anthropocentrism.

At the heart of this synthesis stands the mystery of the Incarnation. God reveals himself in his great sacrament, the true humanity of his Son, Jesus Christ. In his Paschal Mystery, Christ teaches us the true adoration of God, "adoration in spirit and in truth," by his all-embracing love and total commitment to man's liberation and redemption (cf. Jn. 4:23 ff.).

The best example of a theology that is at the same time anthropocentric and most emphatically theocentric is the pastoral constitution *Gaudium et Spes*. Its focus is on man but always in the light of the Gospel. There is no cosmology alongside anthropology, but the whole world is looked upon in the light of man's total calling. "The Council focuses its attention on the world of men, the whole human family along with the sum of those realities in the midst of which that family lives. It gazes upon that world which is the theater of man's history, and carries the marks of his energies, his tragedies, and his triumphs" (*GS*, 2).

The most enlightening and possibly the most extreme case of an anthropocentric theology, which is at the same time

25. John B. Metz, *L'homme l'anthropocentrique chrétienne, pour une interpretation ouverte de la philosophie de Saint Thomas* (Tours: Mame, 1968) and *Moral Evil Under Challenge* (New York: Herder and Herder, 1970). P. Schoonenberg, *The Christ: A Study of the God-man Relationship in the Whole of Creation and in Jesus Christ* (New York: Herder and Herder, 1971). M. Flick and Z. Alszeghy, *L'uomo nella teologia* (Ed. Paoline, Roma) 1971. F. F. Gaborian, *Le tournant théologique aujourd'hui selon K. Rahner* (Paris: Desclee, 1968). P. Eicher, *Die Anthropologische Wendung, Karl Rahners philosophischer Weg.* (Mit einem Galeitwort von K. Rahner) (Freiburg/Schweiz, 1970). The whole theology of Karl Rahner is the most fruitful presentation of an anthropocentric theology, as he himself calls it.

genuinely Christocentric and theocentric, is the image of the last judgment in Matthew (25:31–46).[26] In the Parousia, there will be on the right hand of Jesus among the chosen those who have never come to an explicit knowledge of the name of Christ but, vivified by his grace, have manifested a generous love of their neighbor. For them, the poor discriminated-against fellow man has become the sacrament of salvation, and they have become an image of God's own compassionate love. However, in an era of secularism such as ours, there lurks the danger of misinterpreting this important text in the sense we hear so often in sermons today: "It does not matter whether or not you pray, whether or not you receive the sacraments; the only thing that matters is that you love your brother and commit yourself to justice in the world." These misleading statements do violence to the intention of this sacred text. It neither justifies nor canonizes diverting interest from God to an exclusive interest in man; it answers the question of whether there is salvation for those who truly transcend themselves in unselfish love in search for the ultimate meaning of life although they may not have had the opportunity of knowing Christ explicitly by faith. The whole of the New Testament, particularly the epistle to the Hebrews, deals harshly with those who, having experienced faith in a community of believers, turn away from God and the faith. The text of Matthew, however, also judges severely those who, while still calling themselves Christians and believers, defend every formula of orthodoxy to the point of practically living a heterodox orthodoxy or an orthodox heterodoxy, since they do not put into practice their boasted faith in God, who is the most passionate lover of man.

In the light of biblical texts like that of Matthew 25, we have to approach the shocking reality that, almost two thousand years after Christ's coming among us, the great majority of mankind has not yet come to faith in him. This may include the great numbers of those who call themselves Chris-

26. See Rom. 2:11–16 and the comments I have made earlier in this book.

tians but are not really interested in knowing him and his design for mankind. Thus anthropocentric theology has two main tasks: the first is a most critical self-examination for any hidden atheism or any alienated orthodoxy; the second is to honor God's all-embracing love in those whom some call "anonymous Christians" or implicit believers.[27]

A better expression and more wholesome approach comes from Karl Barth, who speaks mainly of the analogy of faith, *analogia fidei*.[28] The analogy of faith (or implicit faith) is lived wherever man is searching with his mind, heart, and will for that which is good and true—always, of course, with the grace of God. He manifests that openness to the other and a watchfulness for the signs of the times and the real opportunities to do good, that are characteristic of a living faith. Karl Barth would never consider an analogy of faith in a man who has begun to lose interest in God, who locks himself in egotism and pride, or any kind of commitment and interest in man by which he himself would seek self-justification and personal glory. There is an analogy of faith only wherever man, in a self-transcending love and sincere search for ultimate meaning, is truly on the way to the love of God.

It is necessary to emphasize these distinctions because within certain circles today there is a strong tendency to canonize, without process and expense, the whole secular ethics that have severed themselves from faith. The Second Vatican Counsel, while speaking of ethical approaches or systems of thought that do not arise from faith and do not come to the fullness of faith, is most careful to distinguish between "those of our contemporaries who have never recognized this intimate and vital link with God" and, on the other hand, "those who have explicitly rejected it." It leaves no hope for those

27. Karl Rahner often speaks, in his theological essays, of fully alienated atheism on the one hand, and on the other of "implicit faith" or "anonymous Christians." However, he is far from looking on modern atheists and secularists as if all of them were hidden Christians. See P. Eicher, op. cit.

28. See Bernard Häring, *Faith and Morality in the Secular Age* (Garden City, N.Y.: Doubleday, 1973), pp. 157–80.

who have turned away from the God they knew and of whom they have received a valid testimony. However, it speaks with understanding of a strikingly imperfect anthropocentrism: "Some laud men so extravagantly that their faith in God lapses into a kind of anemia, though they seem more inclined to affirm man than to deny God" (*GS*, 19). This anemia could well be a reaction to a too disincarnate theology and to ecclesiastical verticalism. There are, no doubt, many forms of underdevelopment, and if there is no sincere search for integration, they are characterized by decay.

In the struggle against that kind of religion that degraded God to a status of utility, Dietrich Bonhoeffer expressed a thought that later became a slogan: "acting in the world as if God did not exist." The original meaning of these words, in the author's intention, was that Christians should not treat God as one of the many and perhaps superior causalities of the world, but should give man the full freedom and responsibility for acting within his world. Genuine faith never allows any evasion or shirking from responsible initiative.

The same concern is echoed repeatedly by the anthropological theology of Karl Rahner. Our dependence, through faith, on the transcendent God in no way narrows the space of freedom and initiative; rather, it fully activates all the dimensions of autonomy and responsibility within the realm of created nature. Only faith active in love and justice gives us a final orientation and valid criteria for how man comes to his identity and authenticity as steward of the created world.

Bonhoeffer's word can be understood fully only in his own existential situation. It points to the dark night of the spirit when God seems to be far away or almost absent. The man who, in this situation, acts responsibly in view of all his relations to the world, to his neighbor, and to himself, is still in a special way en route to God.

Some "God is dead" theologians, however, gave a totally different meaning to these words. They interpreted Bonhoeffer to mean that the man come of age, the man of the secular culture, will not lose any time with interest in God; instead, he will dedicate himself to his worldly task alone. They claim the autonomy Bonhoeffer had in mind implied that personal maturity that supplants God. Thus autonomy becomes an idol. Man himself will come to replace God and therefore become ever more incapable of transcending himself. Since man is always an adorer, he will be enthralled by his own idols and even restricted in his relationships with his neighbor and with the world, whenever he refuses to take interest in God.

This brings us back to the point of departure in this chapter: the atheist who does not consider God worthy of attention and does not submit the worldly realities to the glory of God, the man who reveals his profound alienation and involves the world, his environment, and his relationship to others in the same alienation. A fundamental option against God in favor of a thoroughly closed system of earthly existence results in an erroneous anthropocentrism, whether individualistic or collective. Thus the power of sin, which is always alienation, is strengthened.

With each mortal sin, man makes himself the center, the measure, the ultimate norm of his own will. We are, however, already touching here upon a very important distinction in mortal sin. We must see clearly and be able to differentiate between the sins of believers and the fundamental option of those sinners who succeed in rationalizing against faith in order to justify the selfish self. These people finally make themselves the center. On the other hand, there is the believer who is driven by passion and by selfishness, who acts against his best convictions while, however, recognizing and truly acknowledging in his innermost being that God's law, which he transgresses, is holy, just, and spiritual. Somehow, in the depths of his being, he still gives glory to God; therefore he is better disposed to return to God in sorrow and in renewed good will than anyone who, through flight into unbelief, tries to justify himself.

15. SOME CONCLUDING REFLECTIONS

It is impossible to synthesize here all the pastoral consequences of the approach to sin that has been outlined. Although we should be always aware that our studies have little value if we lack the courage to follow them through to the consequences, a number of these seem self-evident here. I wish to point only to the main tasks.

The most evident is the centrality of conversion to God in terms of the community and of the unique name by which God calls everyone and summons man to solidarity. It is always a matter of the one call to conversion to God and to one's own fellow man created in the image and likeness of God. The social aspect of the whole reality of alienation, together with the social character of each individual sin, indicate the meaning and direction of true conversion.

Only the Gospel can shed full light on the alienation of the sinful world and the alienating power of each of our sins. All our research would lose its meaning and truthfulness if not carried out with the sincere will to treasure up the Gospel, to meditate on it, and to accept the grace and task of reconciliation.

Our vision of the depth and breadth of sin's meaning as alienation will give some orientation also for the renewal of the sacrament of reconciliation. It is absolutely necessary that we be ever mindful of the social aspects of personal sin. It makes its total investment of alienation in our own being and in the world around us. Consequently, it is indispensable that we integrate the private, individual confession with the various efforts at revision of life and with the communitarian celebration of conversion and reconciliation.

All this must be understood as an important part of the vocation of the Christian to become salt of the earth, light of the world, servant of liberation in his own environment. The redeemed man knows that he cannot return to God alone, yet each of us is truly called in his own uniqueness. Both the personal and the social aspect of conversion and sin are vital; neither can be overlooked.

3

Solidarity of Perdition and Redemption

In all our reflections on sin, one point has become evident: There has been a transition from a rather individualistic concept to one characterized by solidarity. This all-important aspect has to be kept in mind constantly if it is to become the object of systematic consideration. One reason for giving particular attention to this point is the enormous proliferation of books and articles on situation ethics, works still thoroughly imbued by individualism and therefore by one-sided consideration of the individual decision in a framework of self-centered perfection.

No one should overlook the fact that the situation ethics of today inherited its basic individualism from the legalistic style, age-old situation ethics that made null and void God's own law of mercy, justice, and peace in favor of human traditions, customs, and man-made laws.[1] We are forever caught in the vicious circle of discussion on legalism and situation ethics unless we break through to a radical comprehension of man's life as final choice between the solidarity of salvation and the solidarity of corruption. We then arrive at a better understanding of a contextual ethics that considers ethical norms

1. See Bernard Häring, *Morality Is for Persons* (New York: Farrar, Straus & Giroux, 1971), pp. 115-35.

and ethical behavior in terms of the total investment of solidarity, for either good or evil, at a concrete point in the history of salvation.

Man does not make decisions in a vacuum but in the context of his own existential self in the world around him. That world displays a marvelous heritage of goodness, justice, compassion, and authentic reflection invested by mankind, which can only be appropriated in gratitude and with an increased sense of responsibility. On the other hand, there are also horrifying investments of man's solidarity in evil and alienation. These are to be faced and overcome through a very conscious personal choice of solidarity in good, which is the solidarity of salvation.

Individualism falsifies the criteria for personal decisions by blinding man to his important social responsibilities. It allows him an all too easy conscience about the sins of omission. The real dimensions of individual sins are understood in the powerful light of the gospel, which exposes the "sin of the world" and sins within the Church. It seems to me also that we cannot face these problems realistically without seeking a more relevant and integrated presentation of the doctrine of original sin.

1. Sin as Insult to Monotheism and Opposition to Christ

From the very outset, we should keep clearly in mind that one cannot speak meaningfully of the horror of sin or its disruptive power apart from communion with God in Christ and solidarity in Christ. This communion calls all believers together in the battle of faith.[2] The one God and Creator has an absolute right to be honored by all men through brotherhood, kindness, goodness, justice, and mutual respect. Each sin breaks away from this solidarity and thus rejects God.

Christ is the only perfect and absolute monotheist, the ulti-

2. Cf. G. C. Berkouwer, *Sin* (Grand Rapids, Mich.: Wm. B. Eerdmans, 1971), p. 126.

mate solidarity as Savior of all mankind. As brother of all men, he manifests fully the one God, the one Creator and Father of all, and unmasks each sin as opposition to the honor due the one God. One cannot be truly and fully a monotheist, an adorer of the one God, without acting accordingly. Thus faith in Christ, the Savior, and trust in his grace, represent a radical call to a saving solidarity, a coresponsibility for the good, and give us the courage and freedom to fight against our own selfishness and against the sinfulness of the world.

The basic point lies in the truth that each sin is directed against the true and authentic unity of the whole of mankind before the one God and Creator. The solidarity of perdition arising from each sin and affirmed by each sin is all the more terrifying when we consider the full revelation of God in Jesus Christ, who bears the burden of all men and calls us all to unity in the one body and one spirit.

Monotheism is faith in one God, but it is never authentic where it lacks the dynamism toward the solidarity of all mankind before one God. This becomes most evident when Christ's coming reveals God as the one Father of all. His acceptance of our human condition is the very incarnation of that unity that, from the beginning of creation, has been written into the whole history of the world and of mankind.

Already, at this juncture, it should be realized that we do not take as point of departure the biological unity of mankind, or monogenism, as the basis of original sin or solidarity in corruption. A certain desacralization of the biological viewpoint makes way for a stronger resacralization of that brotherhood that manifests the one God, the one Creator, and the one Savior. Without that broader and deeper solidarity, original sin and the sinfulness of the world lose all meaning.

Christ, the perfect monotheist, the Son of God, is the incarnation of solidarity in a way different from all that is already embodied in creation itself and imprinted in the heart of man. The difference is not only quantitative but qualitative and specific: Christ incarnates a solidarity that can never fail.[3] That basic oneness which, by creation through the one God and in one Word is written into the heart of creation, remains open to the possibility of failure but in no way to the necessity of sin. When man, God's masterpiece in the visible created universe, refuses the true solidarity by opting against adoration, against brotherhood, the solidarity will still remain, but instead of being a saving reality, it becomes the expression of corruption and frustration. The created universe, however, which is much more deeply permeated by the inborn dynamism toward a saving unity, will therefore continue to sigh and to yearn for that solidarity in goodness that is perfectly realized in Christ and that should be communicated by the freedom of the sons of God, brothers and sisters of Christ (cf. Rom. 8:18–23).[4]

2. ORIGINAL SIN AND SIN OF THE WORLD

In the course of our reflection, the point will be made, and strongly, that one cannot speak of personal sin, and even less on original sin, outside the basic context of that saving solidarity that is structurally and essentially written into the creation, embodied in Jesus Christ, and continued by the Spirit given by Christ. We have seen how the discourse on original sin can become evasion and alienation. If we consider tradition and doctrine on sin and original sin in the light of the fundamental option between the saving solidarity in Christ and the solidarity in corruption without Christ, we can avoid the danger of fatalism and all temptation to hang the full weight of sinfulness around the neck of the poor first Adam, in order to excuse ourselves.

Furthermore, to concentrate on original sin and on the solidarity in corruption, to the neglect of the infinitely greater solidarity in salvation in Christ, is to falsify the true image

3. Cf. L. F. Shöckel Alonzo, "La rédemption, oeuvre de solidarité" in *Nouvelle Revue Théologique* 103 (1971), pp. 449–72.
4. Cf. H. Mühlen, *L'Esprit dans l'Église* (Paris: Éditions du Cerf, 1969).

of God. It is simply impossible to think that God could, because of the sin of one ancestor, place man under the terrible weight of all the world's sinfulness without offering him an even stronger and all-embracing brotherhood in salvation.[5]

Let us begin our reflection on the basic human choice between solidarity in salvation and solidarity in corruption by examining original sin and a very similar concept, the "sin of the world." These help us to understand more profoundly the social aspect of each personal sin and the gratuitousness of salvation. Much depends, however, on how one presents the doctrine of original sin and on the sinfulness of the world. Where the approach is abstract and severed from the context of salvation history, it becomes a major cause of alienation for many other doctrines.

Revelation and authentic theology speak on sin, particularly on original sin, only in the essential context of the grace of the Covenant, the calling to live in coresponsibility for the salvation of the world, and thus be free from coresponsibility for corruption in the world. Therefore, the fundamental option of one's own life is not centered on the salvation of one's own soul—although surely each individual is called to salvation—but on the final choice for salvation in solidarity with the good, which is offered us by Christ and which alerts us to the horrifying slavery under the solidarity of perdition for those who do not choose Christ.

A discussion of original sin in a treatise of moral theology should not focus on how sinfulness began in the world (*peccatum originale originans*) but rather on the sinfulness we are faced with as a result of all earlier sins which, in classical theology, is called *peccatum originale originatum*. We shall see later how these two aspects cannot be totally separated. Today's hermeneutics disclose that the starting point in the Old Testament was not a direct revelation from God about the first sin of the first Adam. Rather, it is the experience of

5. Cf. I. Schabert, *Solidarität in Segen und Fluch im Alten Testament und seiner Umwelt* (Bonn: 1958).

sin in the world and the threat of solidarity in perdition that forces the inspired authors to meditate also on how sin entered into the world. Since, if man is the image of God, sin cannot be caused by God. So the starting point was that threatening situation that becomes an occasion for the downfall of so many people: the sinfulness that has taken root in cultures, institutions, and nations, and manifests itself in the innermost being of the individual person.[6]

Not only in Israel but in practically all cultures, all existential philosophies, and all religions, man has not been able to avoid the question, "Whence has evil come into the world?" More disturbing than the question of physical evil is the question of the origin of moral evil. Often throughout history, both kinds of evil have been attributed to one and the same source. The confusion of these two different queries causes great danger of giving an explanation that would excuse man and lead to a kind of fatalism. Man could then unload his own responsibility either on an evil spirit or on his ancestors.

The main Christian thesis is that when man sins, he is not a victim of blind fate or of inevitable doom. We should be most careful in our discourse on sin not to allow man to excuse himself through any type of evasion.

The religion of Zoroaster influenced to a certain degree some Israelite thinkers; it also reached Christian cultures through the mainstream of gnosticism and Manichaeism. It gave a full explanation of the existence of physical and moral evil in the world by resorting to a super Satan, maker of the material world and the real cause of all evil. The moral message of the Bible, on the contrary, especially of the New Testament, makes quite evident that sin has its roots in the misuse of freedom, and that there can be no true discourse

6. See Bernard Häring, *The Law of Christ;* in the analytic index, see under "Scandal and temptation," especially in Volume II (Paramus, N.J.: Paulist-Newman Press, 1963).

on sin wherein man is considered unable to avoid it and where no power of liberation is offered to him.[7]

The offer of freedom has its center, its main source, its point Omega in Christ, who is the incarnate solidarity of salvation and thus the Liberator. Wherever man transcends himself in unselfish love and invests in genuine liberating efforts with others, there Christ is present, even if those involved are not conscious of it. Whenever man refuses the solidarity in salvation he is, of necessity, opting for solidarity in corruption and implicitly rejects Christ. This is our main thesis; there is no third choice. Either we choose the one or we come under the other. It is no less a slavery for someone actively to promote such a destructive solidarity. Each individual sin and the sins of groups and collectivities are unavoidably situated in this perspective. Consequently all sins, and not only sins that directly oppose social justice and peace, have an essentially social or antisocial character.

If we approach the question about the essence and chief causes of sin in this way, the figures of Satan and fallen angels can be only marginal. A theology of demonology that casts the devil in the role of chief agent of sin opens wide the door to evasion and self-excuse. Our eschatological battle and all our moral-religious decisions are inserted in the history of mankind, to which we belong. If the serpent, an ultrapowerful personal Satan, would provide the full explanation of sin to the point where it would no longer be a mystery, then we could unqualifiedly excuse ourselves before God and refuse our responsibility.

However, in the perspective outlined here there is room for angels, messengers of peace and goodness, and for demons, in the sense that the horizons of solidarity in good or evil are widened beyond our little planet Earth. Our approach to the question of angels, Satan included, is similar to my ap-

7. M. Flick and Z. Alszeghy, "Il peccato in prospettiva personalistica" in *Gregorianum* 46 (1965), pp. 705–32, and "Il peccato in prospettiva evoluzionistica" in *Gregorianum* 47 (1966), pp. 201–25.

proach to monogenism and polygenism. As I have already stressed, monogenism cannot be the main explanation for a solidarity of mankind in good or evil; and if we accept polygenism as possible or probable, this in no way denies or diminishes that solidarity. It has its source in the fact that all things, all personal beings included, are created by one God. This God is not only creator of the human race on our small planet. In a sense that belongs to the mystery of faith, man's solidarity in good and evil transcends the bounds of our limited human history; yet we find the chief manifestation of the solidarity of salvation on this Earth in Jesus Christ, the Word Incarnate.

In a doctrine concerned with Christian life it seems totally irrelevant to discuss whether angels and demons are absolutely immaterial. This can be of interest only for those who hold an unreasonable and unjust view of the human body. Christ, who has taken a human body and has wrought redemption in his blood, is superior to all angels, whatever their nature may be. We really know nothing about the psychology or social stratification of angels, and it is of no particular interest to us. What does matter is that, before God, there is a mysterious unity of all personal beings, wherever they may be. If perchance man were, in the future, to find other persons on another planet, we would be compelled to take interest in them and to assume coresponsibility with them. Faith in one God, Creator, and in one Redeemer, Jesus Christ, would intimately unite us with them. Since we believe in the communion of saints beyond the Earth, we believe also in communications and therefore cannot exclude any influence between men and angels that might express that unity.

The clear choice of saving solidarity in Christ must free believers from any anguish or fear of Satan. The perspective of solidarity with all of God's friends in the common battle against the solidarity of corruption gives us an additional motive of trust. The main motive is always Christ and the community of faith and love that we experience on earth.

3. THE SIN OF THE WORLD

Christ is recognized and proclaimed by John the Baptist as "the lamb of God who takes away the sin of the world" (Jn. 1:29). The translation that appears in the liturgy, "the sins of the world," is misleading. We are faced not only with the sum total of discrete sins but with that awful power of sinfulness that the Bible calls, in Greek, *hamartia*. It means that solidarity of corruption in which the world finds itself, surely because of all sins but particularly because of some very decisive sins throughout history.

We have been conditioned to think above all of that first sin which, in the course of history, has begun the long series, but we should not forget others that may be more decisive; for instance, consider the sin of that "world" of the religious leaders that rejected Christ and for which Christ, at the end, no longer prayed. That selfish and proud world had closed itself to mercy and grace, to the final manifestation of God's graciousness revealed in Christ. The massive sin of the "godless world" of the Pharisees, the priests, and the lawyers surely has influenced the whole of human history and has completed the sins of the ancestors who have killed the prophets.

The extent to which we keep in mind the mysterious solidarity in salvation and corruption will determine our understanding of the audacious assertion of St. Paul: "Christ was innocent of sin [*hamartia*] and yet for our sake God made him one with the sin solidarity of men so that in Him we might be made one with the goodness of God himself" (II Cor. 5:21). Christ can truly be the reconciliation and the covenant of salvation because he has willed to insert himself into human history in order to bear the burden of the whole of mankind threatened by solidarity of sin (*hamartia*). His saving identification with all men reshaped the burdensome heritage of the past and paved the way to restored solidarity

in salvation for all who will be ready to fulfill his law, namely
to bear the burden of each other (Gal. 6:2). We have to look
behind a certain Jesus image of a newer tradition and experience the realism of the Bible, which provides evidence
that Christ, in the midst of his existence, did experience the
world's temptation (Mt. 4), though only to the point of resisting it and becoming by it, in an even more incarnate
way, the great champion of liberation from sinful solidarity.

In a certain sense, the solidarity of corruption constitutes
the strategic reign of the evil one. Not only is the individual
sin added to the sum total, but it stands in strong interdependence with it. This powerful reign expresses itself above
all in discord, schism, struggle, and hatred. The enemies of
God are united not only by their hatred of God but particularly by their mutual loathing. While they do hate, manipulate, exploit, and curse each other, they are bound in the
same slavery, that of the solidarity of corruption. Where they
join together and agree with one another, it is precisely in the
promotion of evil, enmity, exploitation, violence, and injustice.

Each man is born into a world where, besides the investment of goodness and salvation, there is the horrifying in-
heritance of corruption. It is truly "incarnate"; it is very much
part of institutions, structures, and perspectives that pervert
or block man's capacity to see and to discern. A man born into
a world incapable of perceiving higher values is, in a certain
sense, "born blind." The Council of Trent had many reasons for asserting that original sin, the sin of the world, does
not limit itself to imitation.[8] Man lives in a world of sinfulness, that is, in a family, in a culture, in a social and economic
system where the solidarity of evil is strongly present and
efficacious in varying proportions.

It belongs to man's existential predicament to find himself
in a world which, in many respects, is an incarnate scandal or
incarnate temptation. The situation demands that we rethink

8. Council of Trent, Session V, particularly Denziger-Sch., No. 1513.

the traditional treatise on scandal to free it from an all too individualistic bias. The contaminating power of perverted social, economic, and political structures, scandal as solidarity in corruption must be investigated in order to strengthen both our compassion for the weak and the particular responsibility of the social élites, the call to responsibility in view of the uniqueness of each person in and for the community.

German theologians express the condition of man in a sinful world as *Vorfindlichkeit:* Before and while man is called to make his decision, he is already totally involved in the conflict between the solidarity of salvation and that of corruption. One of the real symbols of this condition is found in the genotype. The chromosomes are bearers of numerous positive and negative characteristics (genes) of one's heritage. These coded informations are mounted and integrated in new directions from the time of conception to birth. This insertion of a being into conflicting and opposing types of solidarity continues through the various influences of the environment, of a world characterized by manifold interdependencies with the whole of history, past and present.[9] At each moment of our earthly pilgrimage, we are surrounded and addressed by the "sin of the world." Nobody eludes the necessity of taking a stand. We should be ever mindful that each individual sin inserts itself in the sinfulness of the world; it increases the solidarity of corruption, the total amount of temptation that marks human history. Those who are hiding and wasting the one, two, or five talents received from God deprive the world in which they live of an indispensable expression of saving solidarity and thus become, consciously or somehow unconsciously, collaborators in the "sinful world."

Our being situated in the world, our being confronted with the sin of the world must not be understood as the total explanation of our own sin. We make ourselves sinners and partners of the sinful world every time we fail to do the good

9. Cf. P. Schoonenberg, "Die Sünde der Welt" in *Mysterium Salutis* II, pp. 886–98.

we could do and commit the evil that could well be avoided. This failure to do good and the capacity to avoid evil must not be considered abstractly but in the total context of our own personal sinfulness—that is, within the framework of the intensity of our own ties with the solidarity of corruption. These bonds originate in our past and present sins and above all come from our lack of sorrow, repentance, and reparation. Whenever we speak on the horrifying reality of sin, the last word is this: We are tied into contaminating collective corruption to the extent that we fail to make our final option for solidarity in Christ, for Christ, the Covenant, Center, and Model of saving solidarity.

So understood, the sin of the world allows no excuse for evasion but becomes a call to total conversion, an explicit change-over to a constructive solidarity possible in Christ only. It is above all conversion from individualism to genuine sociability, to coresponsibility in all that is good. This whole vision makes it clear that it is absolutely impossible to separate individual conversion from our commitment for a more just, more fraternal, and more peaceful world, for better structures and institutions. Above all, it is impossible to sever our conversion from our commitment to the renewal of the Church, so that she may be better able to serve the world.

The biblical doctrine of the sin of the world does not allow us to confine sinfulness to souls only. Certainly we should not underestimate the contamination inherent in perverse attitudes and ideas; they are a jolting reality. But this must never be separated from the whole reality of sin embodied in the culture and in many forms of counterculture, as well as in many political, economic, and social structures and institutions.

Through the power of public opinion, laws, and customs, the given situation holds tremendous sway over those whose justice is superficial and immature. A "justice" that plainly contradicts brotherhood and belief in one God stands as one of the most stubborn obstacles to friendly international relations. Think only that roughly 6 percent of the world's population consumes about 60 percent of the resources of this Earth and make a proportionate contribution to environmental pollution.[10]

The conflict of the world powers, the exploitation of the majority of people and consequent class struggles, terrorism, and violence, the general consumerism hysteria, in the realm of sexuality as elsewhere, all create a reality in man's psychological environment beside which the dreadful pollution of air and water is relatively innocuous. The environmental pollution, the senseless violation and destruction of the resources of our planet are evidently part and parcel of the sinfulness of the world. Its cure will require moral as well as technological effort. The problems of modern ecology can give us a keener awareness of the incarnate solidarity of corruption that manifests itself in a public opinion produced and imposed by artifacts and manipulation, by pressure groups, and by exploiters.

The existential character of man's choice between the solidarity of salvation or that of corruption is strikingly expressed in the Bible, where the whole of religious life is presented as a spiritual battle (Eph. 6:10–20). Paul uses a language often reminiscent of the Old Testament and also of the mythical world vision of his culture. He describes human existence as the great battle being waged in man's environment where he has to face the total power of the sin of the world and of malicious spirits. The real theme is always man's life in his own environment: "The cosmic powers, the authorities and potentates of this dark world" (Eph. 6:12) are not only the legions of fallen angels but more directly and existentially all the human powers, the bearers of authority, and the protectors of the laws who have refused subordination to God, who make themselves independent and exploit others. While authority, laws, and institutions are in themselves good things, often the total sin of the world organizes its energies so as to

10. See *America* (September 30, 1972), p. 229.

use the princes, the authorities, and the power groups of this world in order to perpetuate injustice and increase the immense scandal.

In the Pauline description of the spiritual battle in man's environment, the positive aspect must also be emphasized. Whatever may be the strength of the powers of darkness, the disciple of Christ has nothing to fear if he fastens on the belt of truth, if he puts on integrity as his armor, if he makes himself a messenger of the gospel of peace and justice in all his undertakings and takes up the great shield of faith which will be able to quench all the flaming arrows of the evil one (Eph. 6:13–16). A clear decision for solidarity in Christ is "God's armor"; therefore, in the midst of the battle, the disciple of Christ will give himself wholly to common action, prayer, and entreaty (Eph. 6:18). He will be able to exercise a prophetic role; he will act and speak boldly (Eph. 6:20).

4. THE SINFUL WORLD IN THE CHURCH

By God's grace and calling, the Church is holy; she is the sacrament of saving solidarity in Christ. However, she is situated and lives out her vocation in the midst of a sinful world. While Christ was tempted but never contaminated by the world, the Church is exposed to the sinful world in a very threatening way. She can succumb to the manifold incarnate temptations. Christ, however, gives us the certainty that the Church will not be lacking in protection; Christ's presence will keep her from falling fully victim to the sinful world. Her life will always be marked by visible signs of God's grace and calling.

In order to understand our own participation in the life of the Church and in her calling to be a sacrament of salvation, it is very important to come to a better understanding of how the Church defines herself in view of the sin of the world. Charles Journet advances a theology that was more or less common in the past centuries: "The Church is not without sinners; however, she is without sin."[11] In a true sense, we can assert that it is impossible for the Church to commit sins because only persons can do so. Even if Popes and bishops are sinning, it is not the Church who is the sinner. However, it does not seem to me appropriate to speak on the multitude of sins committed by members of the Church, and even by its officeholders, in such a way as to pretend that the Church herself in her institutional reality is not involved.

I am convinced that Yves Congar gives a much better presentation of the reality when he says that because of the many sins of her members and officeholders, the Church is almost forced to realize her intimate vocation and her desire for sanctity in a historically limited form, which is often far below her calling to perfection.[12] The Church finds herself situated and fulfills her task in the midst of a concrete world. For evangelization, she uses a language and a culture that are, in many ways, contaminated by sin. She adjusts her own life to social structures, institutions, and laws that are impregnated in various ways by the world's sin. By the renewing grace of the Spirit, the Church is always somehow a particular sign of Christ's presence and of his incarnate saving solidarity; nonetheless, sins committed by her members, and especially by the officeholders and communities of the Church, make an investment of this very sinfulness in the Church's own structures. Thus the health and integrity of her visible body is diminished, an unhealthy atmosphere is created, and there arises a temptation of a self-righteous apologetic.[13] In view of the Church's mission to be a sacrament of salvation, this involvement and investment of sinfulness in her own life

11. Charles Journet, *L'Église du Verbe Incarné*, Vol. II (Paris: 1951), p. 904. American translation: *The Church of the Word Incarnate* (New York: Sheed and Ward, 1955). Cf. Charles Journet, *Théologie de L'Église* (Paris: 1958), p. 236.

12. Yves Congar, "Die hailiga Kirche" in *Mysterium Salutis* IV, Part I (1972), p. 469 ff. Also: Y. Congar, *Sainte Église: études et approches sociologiques* (Paris: Éditions du Cerf, 1963).

13. Ibid., p. 471. See what I have said in the second chapter of this book on alienations in Canon Law, liturgy, and theologies.

is, in a certain sense, even more deplorable than the incarnation of the collective corruption in the political, social, economic, and cultural structures of the secular world.

In the past few decades the Church has become much more conscious of the profound interdependence of her own structures, laws, and total health with the world in which she lives. An important pastoral conclusion is that the Church cannot defend herself and live her vocation to holiness, she cannot become a divine milieu for her members, if she does not exercise her saving role in the world and for the world. To understand better the manifold dimensions of the Church's constant need of reform, so strongly reasserted by the Second Vatican Council,[14] and to deepen our understanding of sin in the world, of solidarity in corruption, and original sin, we have to give very special attention to this reciprocal action and influence of Church and world.[15]

Israel, the Church of the Old Testament, was again and again told by the prophets that she was called by sheer grace to become a witness to faith in one God and consequently to a saving solidarity in the midst of all nations. But the sins of the nation, and especially of her religious and secular leaders, often frustrated this mission. Instead of making herself a servant, Israel often inserted herself in the power struggles of the stronger nations and acted with the same mentality as the leading powers. In the decisive hour of the coming of Christ, much of Israel, and particularly its religious leaders, had become thoroughly sinful, and committed the greatest sin in history by rejecting Christ.

14. See *Unitatis redintegratio*, Decree on Ecumenism, Art. 6, where it is explicitly asserted that it is not only a matter of conversion of the individual believers but also one of an ever-needed reform of the Church as institution and in terms of the very way in which she teaches her doctrine and proclaims the gospel.

15. In my book *Macht und Ohnmacht der Religion*, published in 1956 (Salzburg: Otto Müller), I had already treated of this interdependence between the total life of the Church—her institutions, her way of formulating doctrines, and her way of celebrating the sacraments, and so on—on the one hand, and on the other, the total environment, the culture, the economy, the society in which she lives. I shall give further attention to this in the next chapter, where I discuss the theology of liberation.

In the wake of this catastrophe, any discussion on sin of the world has to give full attention to this culmination of collective perversion. It represents not only the sum of all previous sins but also the loss of a unique *kairos*, the irreplaceable hour of salvation. It led to the destruction of Jerusalem, the immense sufferings of the dispersed Jews, the anti-Semitism of so many Christians who did not want to recognize their own share in the sin of the world and unjustly accused and persecuted the generations of Jews who had nothing to do with the crucifixion of Christ. If Israel had heeded the voice of Christ and not yielded to the temptation of violence, her history would have been totally different.

All too often the Church of the New Covenant has followed the example of Israel. Instead of being a sign of unity among the nations, a servant who would lead others to Christ the Servant, she has aligned herself with the power-seekers. Thus the Israels of both the Old and New Covenants have yielded to the desire to dominate the earth.

The key to an understanding of all this is the word of St. Peter, "The judgment begins with God's own household" (I Pet. 4:17). As the schism between Israel and Judah has obscured their witness of faith in one God, the schisms in different parts of Christianity, the pharisaical intolerance, infighting and hatred within the Church, along with domineering attitudes toward the secular realm, jeopardize the credibility of the Church. At least partially, they block her mission to become a sacrament of unity for all mankind and a divine, purifying milieu from which the whole human environment could profit. The sins of Israel were much graver than those of others who were not favored by the Covenant and by revealed truth. On this point, the prophets of Israel are very explicit. In view of the unique grace and calling of the Church, one can say that the most damaging sins taking root in the whole history of corruption are: (1) the rejection of faith in Christ and the refusal to participate in the Church as sacrament of salvation and (2) in a very particular way, those sins opposing an ongoing and profound reform of the Church and leading to ever new temptations to use the Church for one's own self-enhancement and domineering desires. We should do well to remember that according to the Gospel of St. John, the symbol and highlight of the sin of the "world" is the priestly class that refuses Christ, the Servant.

However, if we speak frankly of the sinful world in the Church, we must not forget for a single moment the words of St. Paul that give hope to the whole of mankind, and particularly to the Church, the spouse of Christ: "But where sin was thus multiplied, grace immeasurably exceeded it, in order that, as sin established its reign by way of death, so God's grace might establish its reign in righteousness, and issue in eternal life through Jesus Christ, Our Lord" (Rom. 5:21). Just as we should never speak of the sin of the world, of original sin or solidarity in corruption without extolling the infinitely greater solidarity in salvation, so we should not speak of the Church's shortcomings and need of reform without thanking God for all the miracles of sanctity in her, for all his help in making the Church, in spite of our sins, the sacrament of salvation for the world.

5. Original Sin

Even if the expression original sin has not been used, time and again reference has been made to what constitutes the essence of original sin. It should be evident that moral theology is not interested in all dogmatic questions but in whatever proves useful for human life and the life of the world.[16]

The Bible refers quite often to the *sin of the world* and to sinfulness in the world as expression of the solidarity in

16. Among the numerous books on original sin, I feel that my own conceptualization is closest to that of M. Flick and Z. Alszeghy, *Il peccato originale* (Brescia: 1972). Although my emphasis in a treatise of moral theology would likely be different, I do agree substantially with their vision of original sin.

corruption of those who have rejected the covenant of salvation and faith in Christ, who is the Covenant and thus the Law. Scriptural references to the sin of the world coincide somehow with the essence of "original sin," but not with *peccatum originale originans*, that is, with the question about the first beginning of sinfulness in the world. Passages in the Bible that explore this dimension and allude to the first Adam are rather rare. However, it is not without theological relevance to insist that sin in the world begins historically with personal sin, with a free decision. There is the first Adam and the first Eve with whom the chain of "the sin of the world" began.[17] The doctrine that insists that the first sin was sin in the full and true sense of a personal free decision is most important; it opposes itself to all tendencies that project onto God himself responsibility for the sin of the world. Therefore, all those theories are unacceptable that seek to identify original sin with the primitive chaos and imperfection inherent in the created universe and its subsequent evolution.[18] If one speaks of original sin mainly or exclusively in an evolutionary sense, the dangers of self-excuse and evasion of responsibility increase. A person who does not take seriously the sin of the world, and/or refuses to see it as the result of the many personal sins and solidarity in sin, cannot understand and truly praise the redemption wrought by Christ.

On the one hand, we have to avoid all explanations of original sin that fail to give full attention to the sin of the world and consequently to the necessity of redemption for all men. I expressed a main feature of the doctrine of original sin and redemption when I insisted on "no third choice" between solidarity in salvation in Christ, gratuitous although demanding, and solidarity in corruption. To choose Christ is

17. G. DeFreine, *Adam et son lignage* (Bruges: 1959).

18. The reflections of Herbert Haag (*Biblische Schöpfungslehre und kirchliche Erbsündelehre*, Stuttgart, 1966) have been accused as pointing into this evolutionary direction; see, however, his response: H. Haag, "The original sin discussion 1966–71," in *Journal of Ecumenical Studies* 10 (1973), pp. 259–89.

to opt for his undeserved grace and the law of grace and saving solidarity. On the other hand, there is need to caution against those theories of original sin that attribute to the first Adam and first Eve sole responsibility for our misery in sinfulness. I shall stress the fact that the history of sinfulness began with a free decision of the first sinners, but it is equally if not more important to bear in mind that we all are Adams and Eves when we do the evil that we could avoid and omit doing the good that, by the grace of God, would be within our reach. Above all, those who are in the privileged situation of faith in the Church must be fully cognizant of the social aspect of each of their sins. I subscribe to the opinion of those theologians who assert that the sins of persons who rejected Christ when he came in the flesh, like those committed by persons who have known Christ by genuine witness to Him, are probably weightier than all sins committed before the coming of Christ.

Elaboration of the treatise on original sin in either moral theology or dogmatic theology is anything but an easy task. Good hermeneutics is required for differentiation between divine revelation and that worldview in which it is presented in the Bible. Also needed is knowledge of the various theories that influenced the traditional formulation of original sin, especially since St. Augustine. There are superstructures which, if not properly discerned, can greatly obscure the essence of the doctrine and its meaning for life.

In almost all cultures and religions, there are legends, myths, and reflections in mythological language about the original fall of our ancestors. However, there are two quite different and even opposing ways of approaching the problem. One is fatalistic and pessimistic, thoroughly backward-looking and retrospective. It consequently wastes time bemoaning a lost paradise. Some theological treatises and sermons are not totally free from such an attitude.

The alternate approach, based on biblical doctrine and the best Catholic teaching, is characterized by an eschatological prospect; it is forward-looking. Whatever may be its notion of a lost paradise, the essential message is that all of history is finalized in and dynamized toward the coming of Christ. Everything is geared toward the final liberation and redemption of the world. Initially, perfection exists only as a divine design preparing dynamically for the future.

Only those who accept this vision can take sin seriously and speak of *felix culpa*. Where man recognizes his sinfulness, turns to Christ, and is thoroughly converted to him, man's past sins enter into the future history with a totally new meaning; they become a reason for thanksgiving and for an out-and-out commitment to the solidarity of salvation in Christ.

The biblical doctrine of the sin of the world and the origin of sin, although often presented in the imagery of a worldview that can no longer be ours is, in its essence and dynamics, fully open to a new systematization that takes into account both evolution and the historicity of mankind as experienced today. At the very heart of the matter rests the design of the one God to create a world which, through its inherent oneness, is activated by the Word and dynamized toward the Word Incarnate; in its unfolding revelation, it should make him visible, the one Creator and Father of all. Every gift and grace constitutes a dynamic force and an appeal toward the full realization of his plan. Contrariwise, each sin ostracizes man and tries to block the full disclosure of revelation and bounteousness of salvation. Salvation molds the fully developing man in wholeness and integrity, in coresponsibility, justice, and human peace in view of everlasting beatitude and the communion of saints.

Sin is always decay.[19] If, however, we utilize categories like evolution and development, we then derive their meaning in a context other than the Darwinian or that of a philosophy of history marked by liberalism and Marxism. In our vision, man's freedom lies at the very heart of history. Man is called

19. See Chapter 2, which deals with sin and alienation.

to be a free collaborator of God in history and a corevealer of his love. Misuse of man's freedom, however, renders him an enemy of God and obstructs the history of salvation.

6. CONSEQUENCES FOR MORAL AND PASTORAL THEOLOGY

(a) The centrality of the concept and reality of the *Covenant* in the Old Testament is incontrovertible. Sin takes on its malice and misery with the rejection of the grace of the Covenant. Sin spells ingratitude and loss of all the benefits of the saving Covenant. It not only offends God but imports injustice toward the people of the Covenant.

Theology should return to the great Christocentric vision of the martyr Justin of the first half of the second century who, in his book *Dialogue with Tryphon*, affirms that Christ is the Covenant and thereby stands as our law and orientation. At least fourteen times he reiterates and expounds on the fact that Christ in person is the Covenant and the law.[20] The same line of thought is pursued by many other Fathers of the Church who see in Christ the fulfillment of the Covenant and thus posit as central for Christian life the explicit choice of the solidarity of salvation in Christ. The Church can then easily be understood as sacrament of union with God and of unity with the whole of mankind (*Lumen Gentium*, Art. 1).

(b) In the light of this understanding of the sin of the world and of Christ as Covenant and Law, the vision of the Church as a *divine milieu* becomes concrete and more challenging, for it is precisely at the theological center of the Christians' mission to be light of the world, salt of the earth, yeast in the dough. Moral theology and pastoral efforts are so structured today as to give the greatest attention to the role of the environment in which man lives, and to urge the believers to shape it in solidarity with all men of good will. Christian solidarity goes beyond an appeal to believers to be

20. Jean Danielou, *The Theology of Jewish Christianity* (Chicago: Regnery, 1964), pp. 163–66.

instruments of peace and liberation; it is a whole vision of life, encompassing the moral synthesis that motivates and explains it.

In a subsequent chapter dealing with sins against freedom and liberation, we shall return to this important point. It is of utmost importance that we pay attention to the arduous vocations of the social and religious élite who, in view of their particular role and the gift of God, have been entrusted with the duty of helping all to grow in maturity and co-responsibility.[21]

(c) The vision of solidarity in good and evil also provides a totally new perspective for the traditional treatment and concept of *proximate occasion of sin*. We can no longer ascribe prime importance to warding off occasions of sin. First and foremost comes the mission of the Christian to be a witness in the world, to free himself from selfishness and power-seeking attitudes as well as from distraction and superficiality. Christians are called to share Christ's prophetic role in the world; therefore they need great depth and inner freedom. Salvation must take root in all structures and, above all, must find commitment and zealous efforts on the part of Christians to work with all men of good will for a *healthier environment*, for a more just and brotherly world.

A constructive approach demands a quite different spirituality, an approach that immunizes and makes Christians fit to fulfill their arduous vocation in the midst of the world. This does not preclude the necessity of avoiding morally unhealthy situations and environments, but there is a distinct hierarchy of values. Christians must first accept their mission to be salt of the earth, cobuilders of a better world. This leads to a second exigency, a spirituality capable of preparing them for this task. Third, there remains the duty for certain persons to shun situations that would be too dangerous for them. The danger is not confined to a possible transgression of the sixth

21. See Bernard Häring, *Faith and Morality in the Secular Age* (Garden City, N.Y.: Doubleday, 1973), pp. 181–99.

commandment; we have to stress particularly the innumerable temptations awaiting a selfish man in all fields where he can pursue power and careerism or where he exposes himself to manipulation or any type of seduction. Almost all situations can become dangerous temptations as long as there lurks in one's heart a hidden desire to exploit them for the sake of vanity, individual or group egotism, or any other bad motive. If a Christian frees himself from certain situations, it is not to shirk his responsibilities; he does so in view of collecting his energies so as to prepare himself for the real battle, for the contest of life.

(d) In this same perspective, we also come to a better understanding of the extraordinary importance of *ethical prophetism* in the Church and in the world. The Church has to be the prophetic voice that unmasks ideologies and shatters idols, but the task is impossible if she refuses to discern and to accept gratefully, for her own life, authentic prophetic voices in her midst.[22] A prophet is a person who has both a sense of God and a sense of man. He is characterized by his courage to face the real problems and to denounce lies. However, he is never a pessimist; he does not waste time in useless lamentations. His courage to denounce falsehoods and deceptions—often self-deceptions—assumes real meaning in his resolute and constructive commitment to the common good and his exceptional vigilance for real opportunities to encourage the saving solidarity.

(e) If the vision of solidarity and the sin of the world as I have outlined it is accurate, it becomes urgent to unmask *individualism*, especially when found in the religious-moral field. Individualism of this sort unavoidably partakes of the solidarity of corruption. We cannot rest content with the denunciation of discrete sins of individualistic behavior; we must attack primarily an individualistic vision of the world

---

22. See Bernard Häring, *A Theology of Protest* (New York: Farrar, Straus & Giroux, 1970). See also the document of the Third Synod of Bishops *Justice in the World*, especially the third chapter, "The Testimony of the Church."

and of religion that causes so many sins of omission and of mistaken approaches to fundamental questions. This dimension must be greatly emphasized in our teaching, and more importantly in ecclesial procedures and structures.

For instance, the sacraments are intended to be accessible to our experience and lived as visible signs of solidarity, as a joint commitment to the mission of being instruments of unity, of light and of truth. Each grace, each charism, and each office is given in view of the salvation of the whole world. Therefore any attitude that looks upon grace merely as an opportunity to acquire merits or to perfect oneself is opposed to the solidarity of salvation.

The manner in which we look upon and celebrate the sacraments in this historical moment becomes very decisive. The secular world possesses, in a determined élite, a profound consciousness of solidarity, but it will not know how to connect it with a vision of faith if the whole approach to the sacraments and to other religious expressions fail to manifest that solidarity. A realistic awareness of the danger of secularism, which finds religion altogether irrelevant where it does not shape social responsibility, obliges us to make apparent that the all-important and central sacramental life leads effectively to solidarity rooted in the love of Christ. If rightly celebrated, the sacraments make visible to everyone that it is impossible to abide in Christ's word and love if one does not live in coresponsibility. We celebrate the sacraments truthfully if we mutually reinforce our hope and trust, and give praise to God in community and in view of the needs of the world.

The liturgical reform gives first priority to the communitarian celebration of the sacraments: "Liturgical services are not private functions but are celebrations of the church, which is the sacrament of unity" (*Sacrosanctum Concilium*, Art. 26). "It is to be stressed whenever rites, according to their own specific nature imply that communal celebration involving the presence and active participation of the faithful, this way of celebrating them is to be preferred, as far as possible, to a celebration that is individual and quasi-private" (*SC*, Art. 27). With respect to the *Eucharist*, this vision is generally accepted, although there are still many priests who prefer to celebrate their "own Mass" in splendid isolation, and thereby fail to manifest the Eucharist as a visible sign of the community of faith and solidarity of believers.

Jesus chooses to be baptized as a supreme manifestation of solidarity with all mankind. During a general baptism he receives from John the Baptist that baptism that was, for all the others, a call to repentance and a grace of conversion (Lk. 3:21). He, who is without sin but has come to bear the total burden of mankind, thus expresses the new and perfect justice, the solidarity of the family of God (Mt. 3:15).

The *baptism* he receives from John the Baptist points to his true baptism in his own blood on the cross which, in obedience to the Father, he accepts as the supreme revelation of redemptive solidarity. In the fullest sense, then, he is baptized by the Holy Spirit and offers the total gift of himself to the Father for all of mankind (Lk. 12:50). Our faith in one baptism and one Lord therefore represents a grateful acceptance of that saving solidarity that is the gift of Christ's own baptism. That is why the disciples also are baptized by the power of the Holy Spirit. "The cup that I drink you shall drink, and the baptism I am baptized with shall be your baptism" (Mk. 10:39). "Baptism, therefore, constitutes a sacramental bond of unity linking all who have been reborn by means of it" (*Unitatis Redintegratio*, Art. 22).

Baptism is always an event of the whole people of God, and its celebration should visibly manifest this grace and this commitment. In my eyes, infant baptism is justified if it openly celebrates God's gracious initiative who calls this child to become his son or daughter in the solidarity of the believers. The whole preparation and celebration would then involve that community that joyously and gratefully receives this child as brother or sister. The community commits itself to bring about, by word and witness, a divine milieu, to be a sign and instrument of saving solidarity. If the word proclaimed in baptism is to become a truthful and credible proclamation, there must be a community willing to assure the gradual communication of this Gospel of brotherhood.

If our vision of sin as an outburst and increase of solidarity of corruption is accurate, the *sacrament of reconciliation* must bring out this aspect very directly. The Council stresses the social aspect of the sacrament. "Those who approach the sacrament of penance obtain pardon from the mercy of God for offenses committed against Him. They are at the same time reconciled with the Church which they have wounded by their sins, and which by charity, example, and prayer seeks their conversion" (*LG*, Art. 11). Surely we must not renounce the personal and personalizing aspect of this sacrament, but there is need of an extraordinary effort to free it from the individualistic stamp of the past centuries. To this end, the communal celebration of God's mercy and of our conversion, the communal revision of life, the communal praise of God's forgiveness are essential parts of the renewal of the Church. Karl Rahner has made a heart-searching criticism of the pastoral norms published by the Congregation of the Doctrine, the former Holy Office, on June 16, 1972, because it emphatically denies the sacramental value of communal celebrations and views them only in the perspective of preparation for individual confession.[23]

The Church as a whole is called to ever-new efforts to exemplify in her whole life and in the celebration of her sacraments that conversion and forgiveness that brings about effective liberation from the solidarity of corruption and a better insertion into the community of salvation. Even if the official Church up to now declares the communal celebrations of penance nonsacraments, God can still allow them to manifest his gracious promotion of peace and reconciliation.

23. Karl Rahner, "Bussandacht und Einzelbeichte" in *Stimmen der Zeit* 190 (1972), pp. 363–72.

Through them, God does give many the grace and the calling to saving solidarity. However, this does not stand in contradiction to the Church regulation that whoever is conscious of having committed mortal sins has to submit them to private confession when this is possible.

(f) It further follows that *ecumenism*, the commitment of the official Church and of each believer to overcome the separations of Christian Churches and within Christian bodies, cannot be considered as an optional or superfluous exercise of virtue. A clear vision of the solidarity in salvation versus the threat of collective corruption manifested in schisms, separations, and in-fighting can become for everyone a compelling motive to a firm commitment. The misery of a Christianity torn into shreds and the loveless polarizations within so many Christian bodies result from the sins of all Christians, and thereby press urgently for humble renewal and communal conversion.

(g) May I, at this point, offer some reflections on the dogma of the *Immaculate Conception of the Blessed Virgin Mary*. A new synthesis of any important theological doctrine will always be tested by whether it enriches or impoverishes the understanding of other dogmas. Without attempting to present here a whole picture of the dogma of the Immaculate Conception of Mary, I wish to indicate how the theological approach outlined here can fully evaluate it.

Because of an absolutely gratuitous predestination, Mary is and remains, from the beginning to the very end of her life, free from all contamination by the solidarity of sin. Her life remains a synthesis of praise of God and humble service. Her option for the Servant-Messiah knows no interruption; she is never to be contaminated by domineering attitudes or false expectations of a Messiah as an embodiment of national power. She is the new Eve, the daughter of Sion, who as deaconess (handmaid) is perfectly associated to Christ, the Servant. She thus foreshadows the Church who, in Christ, is to become ever more the new Israel, the servant. She is profoundly conscious that all created reality is the gift of the one God in view of the salvation of all of mankind. She is vigilant for the daily needs of the hour. Because of the superabundance of grace, her fidelity discloses a radical option for the unreserved solidarity of salvation coming from Christ. "Immaculate" refers not only to her soul but to her whole life. The solidarity of corruption cannot reach her since she is perfectly integrated in Christ's own saving solidarity.

4

Sins Against Liberty and Liberation

Manuals of moral theology of the juridical type were interested in the problem of freedom almost exclusively from the viewpoint of whether this individual act met the requirements of a mortal sin. Theirs was an individualistic, static, and isolated consideration about the freedom of an act. We shall have to return to this problem in the next chapter, which examines the distinction between mortal and venial sin. Here our interest is broader: I want to explore all the dimensions of freedom and liberation. Since salvation is freedom and commitment to liberation, sin is growth in slavery.

1. The New Orientation

Any discussion of sin and liberty should avoid two pitfalls. First, it must never create a tendency toward deception. Second, it must not provide occasion for self-excuse and evasion. A guilt complex blocks genuine freedom and blinds people to their real task of growing to their limited but real freedom. On the other hand, there is often the superficial excuse that one lacked full deliberation and freedom, and consequently did not sin. We shall need, therefore, to reflect on the culpable loss or diminution of personal freedom and of freedom for others—individuals, groups, multitudes—through inactivity, apathy in not working to change an environment that is blocking freedom and its development.

We need to be fully aware of the new situation in which our reflections are to be expressed. We are living in a historical moment when the social and religious élites can discern man's calling to commit himself to and engage all his energies in freedom and liberation. There were many things in past eras that were accepted as unavoidable or unchangeable. Today's sophisticated man considers them as an appeal to his creative freedom to change them. We have come to a point where man's right to speak of his own freedom rests solely in his solidarity and total commitment to the freedom and liberation of all.

Through psychoanalytic techniques, depth psychology can free man from many repressions and broaden his conscious and free life by removing the many obstacles that well from the unconscious. Social psychology and mass psychology provide a new key and a sometimes terrifying vision of the external conditions that block or restrict the freedom of many. At the same time, they set directions and open new possibilities for transforming the environment, for creating favorable circumstances for man's freedom.

The new awareness tells us that man can gradually style his psychic life; he can mold public opinion and the spirit of the era. It is within his power to transform social, cultural, political, economic, and ecclesial structures in such a way as to favor the growth of freedom and the increasing awareness that we are all committed to the history of liberation, that we do not want to become slaves and remain in slavery.

Therefore, our treatise on sin is necessarily situated in the perspective of a theology of liberation. I have already explained the essential elements of such a theology by describing the various forms of alienation and by an effort to sharpen the consciousness that only a communitarian commitment to good and liberation can overcome solidarity in corruption that is simultaneously a collective slavery for all those who do not insert themselves actively in the common effort of liberation.

The theology of liberation means nothing to mere spectators. Rather, it reflects the fierce suffering of many as a consequence of those situations and structures that block not only their personal freedom but also that of their fellow man and major portions of society. It is an existential approach that signifies commitment and calls every redeemed man to involvement. The expression of Friedrich Nietzsche "The redeemed should be more redeemed" can be modified to "those who believe in liberation and redemption by Christ should be more thoroughly committed to the growth of freedom and the history of liberation." "The theology of liberation offers us not so much a new theme for reflection as a *new way* to do theology. Theology as critical reflection on historical praxis is a liberating theology, a liberating transformation of the history of mankind."[1]

"The theological expression for nonfreedom is sin. What is meant is not so much sins in the plural but sin in the singular, not so much sinful acts as the sinful state out of which those acts naturally and regularly flow."[2] Lack of freedom offers no excuse for the sinner; it is rather the lack of commitment to freedom and liberation that accounts for the collective sinfulness of the world and the miserable situation of sinners. Each sin stands opposed to the growth of personal freedom and the development of freedom for mankind. Each sin is somehow responsible for oppressive structures, exploitation, domineering attitudes, for keeping people in slavery, for the debasing of ethnic groups and social classes, for the manipulation of public opinion. Although there are very specific sins against freedom and liberation, it has to be said that each sin contributes to the total situation of injustice and exploitation.

1. G. Gutierrez, *A Theology of Liberation* (Maryknoll, N.Y.: Orbis, 1973), p. 15.
2. L. Swidler, *Freedom in the Church* (Dayton, O.: Pflaum, 1969), p. 5.

Nobody can free himself from alienation without committing himself to total liberation.

2. SALVATION AND LIBERATION

From the very beginning, Christ is referred to as Savior and Liberator. The message of liberation belongs to the heart of Paul's gospel: "Christ set us free, to be free men" (Gal. 5:1). Only by a genuine and full vision of salvation intimately united with liberation can we discover the dimensions of sin, particularly sins against freedom.

(a) *A liberating vision of salvation*

A narrow concept of salvation and of liberty provided many occasions for evasion and self-excuse. Freedom can be likened to an embryo with all its potentialities entrusted to man, to the person in community, and to the community of persons. Liberty is a gift of Christ, the Liberator of the community of salvation and of the whole Church. Any individual group or person can truly become a sacrament of salvation by a whole-hearted commitment to the growth of freedom and liberation.

For a theology and pedagogy of liberation, concepts worked out in manuals for confessors with the primary concern of judging the degree of freedom in each individual act are of little or no avail. Instead of wasting our energies determining the quantity and quality of available freedom in a concrete decision, we should center primarily on the task of becoming vigilant for all opportunities capable of freeing man from his egotism and slavery, of developing human conditions that favor the growth of freedom in all. We look to the obstacles to freedom insofar as they can be removed.

There is a great similitude between the concept of salvation and that of freedom-liberation. This affinity was greatly obscured by a disincarnate spiritualism. A most desirable reaction against secularism will reassert that salvation has an absolutely transcendent character; it comprises hope for eternal life in the communion of saints and in the concelebration of God's own freedom. But salvation and liberation are germinally present and are growing realities here in this life. It is precisely this earthly pilgrimage that determines the degree of development or underdevelopment of freedom and salvation. Both are in an eschatological tension between the "already" and the "not yet." This very tension is an invitation to greater freedom, to commit oneself to the full maturity of salvation and freedom on earth.

Israel's liberation from slavery is a real symbol, the beginning of that total liberation promised by the Messiah to his people. It is true that a slave or an exploited worker can obtain eternal salvation. It is equally within the range of possibility that, with the grace of God, and as beneficiaries of the good they have received and still enjoy, they can develop that degree of generous moral freedom that indicates growth toward salvation. However, the man who exploits the slave or the poor laborer, the group that oppresses another, the nation that keeps another in unworthy dependence are not at all on the road to freedom and salvation if they refuse to be freed of their sinful domineering attitudes.

In an era devoid of any real chance of setting slaves free, Paul could exhort them to remain in the social condition in which they came to the Gospel. "Every man should remain in the condition in which he was called. Were you a slave when you were called? Do not let that trouble you; but if a chance of liberty should come, take it. For the man who as a slave received the call to be a Christian is the Lord's freedman, and, equally, the free man who received the call is a slave in the service of Christ" (I Cor. 7:20–22).[3] Whatever may be

3. My translation follows most modern versions, for instance, the *New English Bible*, but there are others who translate: "But even if a chance of liberty should come, choose rather to make good use of your servitude." This translation, to be accurate, must be understood in the social context of the original text, where there was practically little chance for a slave to be freed and subsequently attain an appropriate social status.

the details for understanding this text, one can rest assured that like the whole Gospel, the preaching of Paul introduced a new dynamism of liberation that, at the right moment, must also have its repercussions on the various social structures.

The liberation of Israel from the land of slavery stands not only as symbol of that salvation coming in the other world, but it is also indeed a part of it. Proper understanding of the transcendence of salvation and liberation also includes a firm immanence, a brisk beginning here and now. "The promise of the kingdom of God in which all things will come to justice, to full life, to peace, to freedom and truth does not preclude but includes this time and age. Thus also his love, his sense of solidarity with the neighbor are included; they exclude nothing but rather bring home in hope everything in which God will be everything at the end. The promise of the kingdom is the foundation of the mission in love for the world."[4]

Progressive liberation on all levels—moral, religious, social, cultural, economic, and political—becomes a continuous revelation of salvation wherever mankind commits itself for this liberation. Man then responds to the gift, to the total promise and beginning of freedom that comes from God and will be fulfilled at the end of time.

(b) *Liberty and liberation in history*

The history of salvation cannot be a static reality; it is an ongoing process of freedom and liberation. Man cannot be free and humanity cannot enjoy freedom without a growing and ever-renewed commitment to total liberation. Man's freedom grows in its repeated use, in its constant involvement in and commitment to love, justice, and peace. An act of genuine freedom is always directed toward the growth of freedom and the liberation of all.

Whoever speaks on the history of liberty and liberation

4. H. Moltmann, *A Theology of Hope* (New York: Harper & Row, 1967), p. 159.

cannot restrict his thinking to simple developmental terms. For development to be a key word, the world would have to be removed from the power of sin. Since man lives in a world where, even after the coming of Christ, man is faced with the sin of the world, he is forever confronting the power of sin, that is, a partial lack of freedom and an obstacle to growth in freedom. We must, therefore, go far beyond the categories of development and realize the conflict situation in which man finds himself. If he is to grow in freedom, to work for liberation, it must be while constantly opposing sin and overcoming the obstacles to true freedom. In other words, the moral life of individuals and communities is not merely growth but also an ongoing conversion. Conversion as a response to the gospel of salvation and liberation requires a militant stance against one's innate selfishness and all the investments of evil, in view of ever-greater freedom. Conversion and renewal mean insertion into the total history of liberty and liberation. A social ethics one-sidedly predicated on the concept of development is only veiling the conflict situation by practically denying the power of the sin of the world.

How can we possibly explain the fact that for so long Catholic social doctrine was geared to "development" rather than to "liberation"? The main reason may well be the fear of Marxism and outright condemnation of the fundamental principles of Marxism, namely, the thesis that class hatred is unavoidable. But there can be no doubt that the history of salvation as strife between the solidarity of salvation and that of corruption makes indispensable the assigning of a central role to the idea of liberation. On this point, we see distinctly the progress of thought from the Council document *Gaudium et Spes* to the encyclical of Pope Paul VI, *Populorum Progressio*, and even to the document of the Third Synod of Bishops (Rome: 1971) on justice. The perspective of liberation comes fully to the fore in the documents issuing from the meetings of the Latin American episcopates in Medellin.

There it is unambiguously stated that salvation and liberation in Christ become for all Christians "a mission for the liberation of all men from the slavery in which sin, injustice, and hatred keep them and which find their origin in man's egotism."[5] The liberating salvation granted us in Jesus Christ asserts itself in intense continuity and deepens with everything that is good and just. But, it also introduces rupture and discontinuity with everything that is sin or the result of sin; thus it really does become a fight against alienation in all its forms, especially the type of estrangement brought about by institutionalized temptations.

(c) *The liberation of imprisoned subconscious forces*

Teilhard de Chardin believes that the dynamics of hominization lead to the development of the highest possible forms of consciousness. Christ is the point Omega because he is the very presence of the Word in the ongoing creation and hominization process. Everything points to the Word Incarnate who is fully conscious of both his coming from the Father for all men and his going home to the Father with all his redeemed (freed) brethren.

Psychoanalysis, through its techniques of free association and fantasy analysis, discloses to us heretofore unsuspected forces. It broadens the space of the conscious self by freeing it from all the experiences which, up to now, have been imprisoned in the impersonal *id*, that is, in the subconscious-unconscious realm, which so often blocks personalization and the growth of freedom. Genuine therapy seeks to remove whatever limits the unconscious self in the exercise of its freedom. The therapeutic process amplifies the conscious sphere by lifting from the unconscious-subconscious the most troublesome repressions. The great merit of the logotherapeutic school of Viktor Frankl lies in the clear intuition that these newly liberated forces can insert themselves in the history of genuine human health and salvation only to the

5. Document *Justitia* (Medellin), Art. 52.

extent that man acquires a new freedom to search for the ultimate meaning of his life and yearns to live accordingly.[6] Expansion of the conscious self serves true freedom to the extent that it disengages man from a vague introspective self-consciousness. Psychoanalysis stands as a liberating force when it situates itself in that consciousness of freedom for which Christ has set us free. It then becomes a promising possibility; it appeals to the realization of one's personal freedom together with and through commitment for the freedom and liberation of all.

"At almost the same time, psychology was uncovering the profound importance to the individual memory, conscious and unconscious in the perception of current reality, and the liberating force of the act of transferring knowledge from the unconscious to the conscious memory, history was making somewhat similar findings for communities."[7] It is now possible to compare particular modern situations with earlier or contemporary cultures through the historical method. The behavioral social sciences promote the comparison of cultures and thereby offer man new possibilities for responding to modern needs without allowing the latest traditions to enslave him. The immobilism and lack of freedom of traditionalist movements are usually rooted in their lack of knowledge of the broader tradition in its totality. The temptation is real to absolutize the very latest addition to any ossified tradition.

A timely example can be seen in recent development relative to the sacrament of penance which, for instance, in the "pastoral norms" issued by the Congregation for Doctrine (Rome, June 16, 1972) on the subject of confession and general absolution, presuppose a rather narrow understanding of the doctrine and legislation of the Council of Trent and an abiding validity of the various decrees of the Holy See

6. Bernard Häring, *Medical Ethics* (Notre Dame, Ind.: Fides, 1973), pp. 172–80.

7. Swidler, op. cit., p. 14.

through the seventeenth and eighteenth centuries. The document also assumes that the traditional distinctions between mortal and venial sins constitute integral parts of future developments. Therefore, the norms fail to come to grips with the variety of traditions in the Church, including the Church's broader vision of sacramentality, her fight against particularly scandalous sins, the interdependence between her self-understanding as a great sacrament of conversion and humble confession in life, repentance and liberation, and a pluralistic evolution of the sacrament of reconciliation throughout the first thousand years of its history. The aforementioned article of Karl Rahner assesses this decree as lacking strikingly in awareness of the new situation as well as misjudging past history.

The new form of historical consciousness enters into the perspective and dynamic of salvation and liberation history when integrated in the *Eucharistic memorial*. In the Eucharist the great events of the history of salvation come to our conscious memory. We experience the liberating opportunities of the present moment in that vigilance that is the fruit of gratitude for God's gifts of the past, of the repentance for our past sins, of hope and of responsibility for the future. The man of today cannot celebrate the past events of creation, of the incarnation, death, and resurrection of Christ without a more lively consciousness of the present *kairos* in relation to the whole of past history. The Eucharistic celebration wants to extend our total vision of history in order to give us a greater freedom in openness to the present opportunities, especially in the fight against obstacles to human and Christian liberty. The memorial of the death and resurrection of Christ offers the broadest horizon for a liberating consciousness of human history. If, in this historical moment, parts of the Church refuse full acknowledgment of the greatness and shortcoming in past history, they cannot credibly celebrate the Eucharist for modern man, because we are called to enter in an incarnate way into that liberating memorial of the history of salvation.

(d) *The liberty of the sons and daughters of God, and liberty expressed in the human situation*

The freedom for which Christ has redeemed us is liberation from selfishness in the service of the neighbor, to the praise of God. Since it is the gift of the Word Incarnate and of the Spirit who renews the face of the earth, this inner freedom cannot be grasped in its spiritual and transcendent dimensions unless freedom becomes an incarnate reality in the human situation. A vague vision of a world yearning for a share in freedom does not suffice today; we have to confront the freedom of the children of God with that better knowledge, that scientific approach that history, sociology, psychology, and all the modern social sciences allow us.[8]

Man's innermost freedom is strictly interdependent with his physical and psychological environment. Today we can understand better how our destiny is the outcome of the freedom of the many; hence it appeals to all, especially to the social and religious élites, to work for greater liberty in their environment, so that the spirit of human and Christian freedom can take root there.

It would be misleading to think of environmental influences and social evolution as mere limitations on human freedom. Our different types of environment demand the promotion of all possible opportunities for human freedom; of course, they also set limits to our collective and individual freedom of choice as well. The milieu not only favors or limits the freedom of the individual in his personal way of life but also opens ever-new horizons of the individual and communal growth of freedom in relation to the social world around us. "The opportunities offered to human freedom to

8. Cf. G. Gurvitch, *Déterminismes sociaux et liberté humaine* (Paris: 1955) and *La vocation actuelle de la sociologie* (Paris: 1957). Also Bernard Häring, *Marriage in the Modern World* (Paramus, N.J.: Paulist-Newman Press, 1965), pp. 33–70.

intervene creatively in social reality vary considerably with variations in the social situation and structures. This situational freedom (*liberté située*), freedom within the framework of things as they are, this relative and conditional freedom inseparably linked to the individual and collective human situation whose extent is very variable, has its strength and scope increased or diminished according to the social type of the smaller and greater groups, and of the over-all global structure."[9]

Scientific investigation of sociological determinisms and processes in no way implies a denial or endangering of freedom, but it can point out the admittedly limited but nonetheless real opportunities for human freedom. It can reveal how personal freedom can join forces with the community in such a way that the sociological determinisms and processes will serve freedom. "Human freedom is dependent upon making use of the various determinisms as cardinal points and as means of intervening in the course of events. Above all, human freedom makes use of sociological, biological, and psychological determinisms and processes in order to reach its goal."[10]

The measure of our freedom is contingent, to a great extent, on the amount of well-applied freedom we have invested and/or are continually reinvesting in the shaping of our milieu and over-all social structures. Society as a whole, its social classes, its various groups and individuals create their own fates through the different ways by which, in every situation and in every context, they deal with prevailing environmental forces, bend them, overcome them, take them in hand, and make use of them. They are thus unremittingly creating and shaping their own characters by changing the milieu in which they live. Our environment is the material of our creative liberty and a main object of our commitment to liberation.

9. Gurvitch, ibid., p. 2.
10. Ibid., p. 82.

Freedom is not entrusted to isolated individuals but to persons as members of a community and to the community itself. Its growth is a function of solidarity. This principle is of exceptional importance in the present age with its intricate collective ties and the pressure of mass organizations. It is futile to attempt fighting the impersonal collective and its inherent dangers to moral freedom with a freedom that cares only for the individual. We therefore need a new pedagogy of freedom. Everyone should realize fully that liberty derives its strength primarily by taking form in the social life and environment in which we are called to develop our own freedom and promote the freedom of others.

The pedagogy of freedom calls for integrated communities. In the long run, a personal choice of freedom can withstand the forces embodied in oppressive systems and misleading ideologies only if it finds expression in a community actively committed to the shaping of the world around us. Even a man of good will needs the life environment and example of a community in which good has taken form and that supports and invigorates his freedom. A pedagogy of liberty and liberation should emphasize personal responsibility in shared experience, coreflection, and common commitment. Further, in a pluralistic and extremely dynamic society, freedom needs to be given greater immunization and a greater depth by a more lively perception of values and scale of values. Freedom especially needs to be sustained by a spirit of solidarity.

The precaution of flight should take last place in our approach. There are circumstances where there may be an urgent obligation to flee from a noxious environment; it may be that it represents a proximate occasion of sin because the combined efforts of all men of good will cannot remove the deleterious factors. Just as there are strong characters who bear the main burden of humanizing any milieu, there are also the weak, those who, as yet, are not sufficiently immunized. If, however, salvation by flight became predominant in people's minds today, such a situation would ultimately

lead to desertion by the élites. The basic principle of a pedagogy of liberation is that nobody can preserve his own freedom and integrity without inserting himself in the common
effort to create liberating structures and a more humane environment.

(e) *A holistic vision of freedom and liberation*

Although I am ready to accept some points of the analysis
of Karl Marx, my total vision of freedom and liberation is
diametrically opposed to his doctrine of alienation. Because
Marxism has not believed that social and political changes
must go hand in hand with the creation of a new man, a new
spirit, all Marxist revolutions up to now have only led to
more oppressive forms of state capitalism, and domineering
if not immobile bureaucracies. History testifies to the fact
that violent revolutions usually install new and even more
violent oppressors. True liberation comes from a long and
patient process that cannot be achieved by a *coup d'état*, by
a sudden and violent overthrow of the existing political
machine. I would not want the reader to conclude that we exclude from our consideration any effort to eliminate an unfit
and oppressive government. However, the best of Christian
moral theology has always tried to propose a synthesis of
individual conversion and the reshaping of structures, institutions, public opinion, and the like. The liberation of mankind
is the work of each person and each community. It must
always contend simultaneously with the obstacles arising from
one's personal egotism, from group egotism, group pressures,
and obstacles arising from immobile structures. If we wish to
speak of a liberating revolution in realistic terms, we will
make sense only if we come to a holistic vision of the macro-
and microsocial reality with its internal and external forces.[11]

Israel's exodus from Egypt becomes a saving event because
of the rupture with past servitude. It happens in an atmos-

11. Cf. D. Cooper, *Introduction to S. Carmichael, et al.: Dialectics of
Liberation* (London: 1968), pp. 9–10; Gutierrez, op. cit., pp. 25–27.

phere of the Covenant and becomes for each member, each family, and each group a grace and a task to create a new people, a people with a new heart.[12] Like the biblical concept of *shalom*, peace, the concept of salvation and liberation is of an equally unique wholeness. Man can accept this gift and accomplish his task only in this perspective of wholeness. If in the past, morals often yielded to the temptation of spiritualistic evasion, we have now to resist a perverse liberation as, for example, that of Marxism. We must reject the unfounded hope that people can be freed by structural changes and violent revolution alone.

The liberation that is a gift of God and a calling to total commitment in solidarity is a long process. Hope for its immediate realization can only be a false messianism and a new form of alienation. The freedom for which Christ has redeemed us and that gradually realizes itself in the solidarity of salvation means "being in becoming," being ever more free for the selfless love of others, a constant effort to incarnate the liberating force of faith and hope in the structures, institutions, public opinion, and totality of our human environment. The commitment for complete liberation presupposes leaving behind our ingrained selfishness while, at the same time, combating all those structures that keep us in servitude. The total liberation we are striving for is based on unconditional openness to others. "The fullness of liberation—as a free gift from Christ—is communion with God and with other men."[13]

(f) *The Church as sacrament of liberation*

Christ alone is the perfect sacrament of freedom and liberation. In Christ, the Light and Liberator of all nations, the Church is called not only to celebrate the freedom of the children of God in communion with him but also to become more visibly and effectively a sacrament, that is, an instru-

12. A. Gelin, Moise, *L'homme de l'Alliance* (Paris: 1955), p. 39.
13. Gutierrez, op. cit., p. 36.

ment and promoter of liberation for all men. The Church cannot be, as *Lumen Gentium* expresses it, "a sacrament of union with God and of unity with mankind" unless she accepts her role to be a sacrament of liberation in the actual situations of conflict that arise in life. This consciousness of her mission will thus gradually inscribe itself in the entire life of the Church, in all her structures, in her celebration of the liturgy, and in her moral message and pedagogy, so that these really become a morality and a pedagogy of liberation. The revision of Canon Law, too, must be tested in this light.

It would be interesting to study the Second Vatican Council and the postconciliar Church in this decisive perspective, especially in view of the constitution *Gaudium et Spes*, which represents an admirable effort of the Church to free herself from all kinds of ecclesiocentrism on the level of her structures. The renewal of the Church, in the sense of genuine liberation, can be achieved only by her fully understanding herself as a servant of the world in which she continues her pilgrimage. We have come to a deeper realization that in ecclesiocentrism, and equally in too great a desire for direct or indirect power over the secular sphere, there is serious danger of alienation and of partial loss of the charism of the Church to become an ever more effective instrument of liberation.

The Church of the Poor means humility, the breaking of any alliance with the powerful and the rich, and humble gratitude for God's gifts, which become instruments of generous service for the liberation of the poor and all those who are oppressed, manipulated, and exploited. This is the way to proclaim the kingdom of God, which is close to the poor.

The Church's mission to be and to become ever more an instrument of liberation is greatly helped by the declaration of the Second Vatican Council on religious freedom. We have become keenly aware that faith is a liberating power only if received in full freedom. The Church becomes a sacrament of salvation and liberation only if she puts her trust, not in the secular arm or in the help of the powerful, who so often are oppressors, but thoroughly in the liberating force of the gospel and the testimony of Christian life and liberating Church structures.

The first encyclical of Paul VI, *Ecclesiam Suam*, with its main stress on dialogue, is a great document on the Church as a sacrament of liberation. Genuine dialogue means, above all, a readiness and capacity to listen. It means accepting the total word that comes from reality, in constant readiness to learn, to come to a better understanding of man in order to proclaim the gospel more effectively.

Christ the Liberator is the servant Messiah announced by the second Isaiah: "The Lord God has given me the tongue of a teacher and skill to console the weary with a word in the morning; he has sharpened my hearing that I might listen like one who is taught. The Lord God opened my ears and I did not disobey or turn back in defiance" (Is. 50:4–5). The Church of Christ the Servant, the Listener and the Dialogue, can be a teacher and consoler of the sufferers only to the extent that she, too, "listens like one who is taught." She can be a liberating force if she is outstanding in promoting the dialogue and in discerning and accepting the prophetic voice, so that she herself can be a prophetic and liberating voice in the world.

The readiness of the Church to engage in dialogue—that is, always to listen respectfully to the secular world, to the non-Christian religions, and particularly to the separated Christians—is in itself a liberating event. Dialogue with the Greek Orthodox Church, and with all those churches that have issued from the reform groups of the sixteenth century, represents a readiness to integrate within our own Church those parts of the common heritage that they have not only conserved but have developed in a particularly successful way. Ecumenical dialogue not only tends to communicate our truth better but also demonstrates our willingness to receive the message and to correct our errors and narrowness. Dialogue with the world, even when that world tells us uncomfortable truths, is a way of listening to the Spirit who is present in the whole of human history and who works in all, through all, and for all.

The Church is surely expected to use discernment, gift of the Spirit, but this is not possible if she is not ready to learn, to unlearn, and to renew herself. Refusal to learn from those who are outside the Roman Catholic Church is nothing less than a sin against the Spirit. "Of what greater sin can a Christian be convicted than refusing to harken to the Spirit?"[14]

An all too easy and superficial apologetics, combined with resentment against the Orthodox and Reformed Churches, became serious obstacles to the internal freedom of the Catholic Church. We remember, for instance, how anti-Protestantism made the Catholic Church so long reluctant to introduce the vernacular in her liturgy, to open the Bible fully to the people, and to examine her own structures and ministries. Anyone who understands the profound meaning of dialogue between the churches and between the Church and world will be astonished by the profound interdependence of freedom, reparation, and dialogue. "It is no accident that freedom and dialogue are associated in so many ways and in so many places."[15]

3. THE MORAL MESSAGE OF THE BIBLE: THE BASIS OF A THEOLOGY OF FREEDOM AND LIBERATION

In the following pages I try to deepen and broaden what has already been said about the relation between salvation and liberation, as well as to draw the fundamental lines of a moral theology whose chief perspective is liberty and liberation.

(a) *Liberation through the law of faith*

Monotheism, faith in one God, Creator of all men and of all things visible and invisible, enters into the history of Israel

14. L. Swidler, op. cit., p. 60.
15. Ibid., p. 61.

as a unifying and liberating force. This faith desacralizes all the taboos and myths that deprived man of the free exercise of his stewardship over the world. Man, made in the image and likeness of his Creator, becomes aware through faith that all creation is entrusted to his freedom, and that no other limits are imposed on him than the good of man himself: "man" understood as the whole of mankind, the family of God that honors God, the one Creator, when it frees itself from all selfishness and administers the earthly goods and its own capacities in creative fidelity. With the growth of her faith in one God, source, center, and goal of the whole creation, Israel comes to understand better her role as witness and instrument of freedom and unity among the nations. Faith thus manifests the profound interdependence of solidarity in salvation and total liberation.

Christ, the absolute and perfect Monotheist, who comes from the Father and returns to the Father, tears down all obstacles to absolute unity and the solidarity of mankind. Paul, apostle of Christian liberty, rejects those Jewish laws, traditions, and even the formulation of moral imperatives that might obscure that faith in the one Father and Redeemer. He proclaims the message of a liberating faith. Christ is not servant of the law or of Israel. Rather, faith in him, the unique Redeemer and Liberator, adds a new dimension and a new dynamic to morality, calling all believers to live the Paschal mystery by dying to their selfishness and rising to a new life. Faith in Christ, which justifies through grace, provides the authentic criteria for discerning what is good in the traditions and customs of a nation and culture.

The law of faith proclaimed by Paul reveals Christ as the one who challenges the sacralized egotism that would separate Israel from the other nations and cultures. It allows no superiority complex or discrimination against others. "Do you suppose God is the God of the Jews alone? Is he not the God of Gentiles also? Certainly of the Gentiles also, if it be true that God is one. And he will therefore justify both the circumcised in virtue of their faith and the uncircumcised through their faith. Does this mean that we are using faith to undermine law? By no means: We are placing law itself on a firmer footing" (Rom. 3:29–31).

A morality thoroughly based on faith in one God and in one Liberator, Jesus Christ, does not allow any nation to exploit another, does not allow any culture to despise others, nor men to domineer over women (cf. Gen. 3:16), since they are equally created in the image of God.

Once it is understood that faith is not an ideology or a mere speculation, but total acceptance of God's self-revelation, and gift of one's self, the whole morality based on faith becomes liberation for true solidarity and brotherhood in justice and peace.

Faith is a joyous and grateful acceptance of the gladdening news, and this means liberating news. The joy of faith brings with it that inner freedom that is the premise and dynamic of nonviolent commitment to one's own liberation and that of others. If faith does not become feast, joyous celebration, it is not authentic and will not sustain the full liberation.[16]

Faith is an event of salvation and liberation only if it remains a joyous acceptance and a serene and grateful commitment to solidarity in salvation and liberation. The Church has to be as much concerned for that joyous aspect of faith as for the right formulation of the articles of faith. Whoever gives priority to mere orthodox propositions, and even to cold and militant teachings, to the detriment of joyous faith, or whoever gives first place to law, even moral law, deprives faith of its liberating force. He makes of morals a closed system that allows and encourages all kinds of evasions, and justifications for inertia, discrimination, and even exploitation. If, on the

16. Harvey Cox, *Feast of Fools* (Cambridge, Mass.: Harvard University Press, 1969). This book represents quite a change in emphasis and perspective in comparison with his earlier work *The Secular City* (New York: Macmillan, 1965). See also: Jürgen Moltmann, *The First Liberated Man in Creation: The Theology of Play* (New York: Harper & Row, 1972) and *The Future of Hope* (New York: Herder and Herder, 1970).

contrary, morality arises from joyous faith as the liberating message of the gospel, if faith in one God, Father, and Liberator motivates our whole moral approach, then nothing will ever obstruct the freedom of the spirit. Morality then becomes a liberating commitment to the whole of mankind.

(b) *The liberating force of hope*[17]

Hope was thoroughly emasculated and deprived of its liberating force by those manuals of moral theology which, in past centuries, were concerned chiefly with the stability and security of "throne and altar": the establishment. In striking contrast, the renewal of the Second Vatican Council and of the postconciliar era gives a very important role to Hope.

Hope is the dynamic force of that faith that believes in the God of history who was, who is, and who will come. It is trust and gratitude for all that God has done in history, which guarantees for all time his gracious and liberating presence. Thus, while assuring us of the future, it draws our attention and our energies to the *now*, the *kairos*, the time of our present opportunities. Hope grants us the courage to accept the historical material and opens our eyes to all its potentialities. It is also a call to renewal, a summons to shape and reshape the past that we have inherited, with a view to gradual liberation in the service of the future.

Obviously, this concept of hope has little in common with that narrow approach that is concerned with one's personal salvation alone. Individual salvation is, of course, a legitimate concern, but if it is isolated from the whole context of salvation and liberation, it becomes a deadly and disintegrating force. I refer again, as a shocking example, to Calvinism's poisonous fruits in the shameful discrimination against blacks in North America and the horrible alienation in the Dutch Reformed Church of the Afrikaners. Their concern for in-

17. I here synthesize briefly what I have developed at greater length in my book *Hope Is the Remedy* (Garden City, N.Y.: Doubleday, 1972), particularly in Chapters 3, 4, 6, and 13.

dividual salvation, with material success as the criterion, thoroughly destroys the hope of unity and solidarity under one God, one Father, one Liberator, Jesus Christ.

In his epistle to the Ephesians (4:3–6), Paul introduces his vision of hope with the words, "Spare no effort," and thereby alerts us to the sins against hope and liberation: "Spare no effort to make fast, with bonds of peace, the unity which the Spirit gives. There is one body and one Spirit, even as there is one hope held out in God's call to you; one Lord, one faith, one baptism; one God and Father of all, who is over all and through all and in all." It is that hope-in-solidarity described in his epistle to the Romans, where all the created universe is sighing and yearning for a share in the liberty of the children of God, that final liberation from the solidarity of corruption (Rom. 8).

Christian hope, arising from the gift and promise of the messianic peace and liberation, opens wide all horizons for personal and communal growth in liberty. It is from want of true hope in a world that has lost its sense of purpose that all the vanities of self-enhancement and the miseries of alienation from self and from our fellow men flow. The mission of the Christian community is to restore to this world those dimensions of the future that appear in Christ crucified and the risen Christ.[18] Hope is the mission of believers to give back to the world the liberty to serve, the liberty of true justice and peace.

In a certain sense we can accept the thesis of Harvey Cox that the only future of theology lies in the conversion of theology to the future.[19] However, more than Harvey Cox and Moltmann, I would emphasize gratitude for all that God has already revealed and granted to us. Thankfulness for the past, including human tradition, and trust in his promises call us all

18. Jürgen Moltmann, *Theology of Hope* (New York: Harper & Row, 1967), p. 338.

19. Harvey Cox, *On Not Leaving It to the Snake* (New York: Macmillan, 1967), p. 12.

to responsibility and coresponsibility in the present moment, as servants and corevealers of the hope of the future.

This alertness to the present moment guarantees the fullness of hope that never allows any evasion or wishful thinking. What future generations will expect from us is, above all, that we shall have used to the full our present opportunities (cf. Eph. 5:15) and tried to understand God's will, always keeping in mind the full dimensions of the past, the present, and the future.

Christ is the Prophet, the fulfillment of the prophetic message and total promise of the beatitudes. His prophetic proclamation of salvation and the witness of Christian hope is a promise of final liberation that can never be dissociated from commitment to the liberation of the poor, the minorities, the migrants, and those individuals and groups who are victims of discrimination.

The alienation caused by individualism, overprivileged social classes, and the "high clergy" of the Constantinian era has often in the past obscured the dynamic liberating force of the beatitudes. Christ is the hope of the poor and of the prisoners because he has come to make them free. His gospel is a most urgent invitation to his disciples to join in his prophetic mission. "The Spirit of the Lord is upon me because he has anointed me; he has sent me to announce good news to the poor, to proclaim release for prisoners and recovery of sight for the blind; to let the broken victims go free, to proclaim the year of the Lord's favor" (Lk. 4:18–19; also Is. 61:1 ff.).

If the high-ranking clergy and the pious capitalists consoled the poor only with the hope of a transcendent future, with happiness for their souls in another world, their proffered solace was plain lie and alienation. The hope that Christ proclaims in the beatitudes is truly a transcendent one—a promise of total liberation at the end of time—but it provides also the dynamics for the here and now by its resounding call to his followers for liberating action in this time and age.

Renewed by the Spirit, the followers of Christ realize the

genuine meaning of "poor in the Spirit"—that everything is gift of the Father and cannot be enjoyed unless it draws people together in one Spirit and becomes service and commitment to the poor. For those who live in misery and discrimination, for those who are exploited, the kingdom of God is a promise, a present assurance that all who have accepted it will join forces to liberate the oppressed.

Christ is the great sacrament of hope because, with his coming, the process of liberation becomes more visible and urgent. Although its fulfillment must await the second coming, the sign of the kingdom's presence and the hope of its fulfillment is there; the liberation is actually going on. Therefore Jesus answers the disciples of John the Baptist, "Go and tell John what you hear and see: The blind recover their sight, the lame walk, the lepers are made clean, the poor are hearing the good news" (Mt. 11:3–6).

The coming of the kingdom of God, and the hope that Christ proclaims in the beatitudes, make possible and urgent an ongoing conversion. They call for a radical transformation of ourselves and the readiness to be involved in the process of liberation of the poor, the exploited, the underdeveloped, in a realistic and wholehearted way, not only with monetary assistance but also with clear analysis of the situation and a corresponding strategy.[20]

The great document of the French episcopate on the Christian's involvement in politics, approved on October 28, 1972, stresses lucidity and rigor of analysis but gives equal importance to that constructive intuition and imagination that frees us from bondage to the previous day's analysis.[21] "Certainly the Christian's option is not one of tranquillity. Faith urges him to prefer an imperfect secular city to one that is more imperfect. He is aware that this commitment remains necessary to the end of time, since a marvelous great society—one integrally transparent and totally fraternal—will never

20. Gutierrez, op. cit., p. 194.
21. *Documentation Catholique* (November 19, 1972), pp. 1011–26.

be fully realized. He knows, too, that politics, like any other human reality, has to fight against the mystery of evil. This diagnosis does not discourage Christians. Hope allows them to live, to act, to fight, without the need for the opiates of illusion and simplifications."[22]

To neglect or obscure these aspects of Christian hope is not only a sin against hope itself but also a sin against our full freedom and our mission to align ourselves with Christ, the Liberator.

(c) *The liberating dynamics of grace*

The Spirit renews the face of the earth and so vivifies the ministry and testimony of the Church. It brings not only life but also liberty and the mission to be coredeemers through his liberating grace. "Where the spirit of the Lord is, there is liberty" (II Cor. 3:17). True believers can wage the battle against evil, against the concupiscence of the world, and against temptations that arise from their own egotism, because they are reborn by the Spirit; they put their trust in his renewing grace and not in themselves (cf. I John 3:14).

It is the Spirit who gives a new heart and a new life so that men can love with a liberating love. Because of this trust in the Spirit, the word of God abides in them (I John 1:12). The Spirit gives them truthfulness, which opens them to the liberating truth and urges them to act on it (Jn. 16:3). Believers, like others, are tempted by the sin of the world, but because they experience the renewing power of the Spirit, they act according to truth and live according to the gift of redeeming love, trusting that "no child of God is a sinner; it is the Son of God who keeps him safe, and the evil one cannot touch him" (I Jn. 5:18).

The liberty given by the Spirit to the sons and daughters of God brings forth generosity, spontaneity, and creativity, not only for their personal self-realization but equally for the

22. Ibid., pp. 1020–21.

union of all men in an ongoing effort for liberation on all levels.[23] The grateful knowledge that we are "no longer under law but under grace" (Rom. 6:14) is an experience so liberating that it transforms our attitude and mentality and gives us an intuition of the utter gratuity of redemption, salvation, and freedom. The very gratuitousness of God's graciousness then becomes the norm of our life.

True believers realize more and more that not to use the talents God has given us is an offense against the Creator and against the Spirit who distributes the multiplicity of his gifts in view of man's solidarity in liberation. The love that knows itself to be a gracious gift of the Spirit overcomes the egotism incarnate in the old Adam and in the world around us, which, however, is yearning for a share of his generous love and justice. Those who live under the influence of the gifts of the Spirit soon see the whole of creation, and especially their own capacities and material goods, as gratuitous gifts of God, a vision goes far beyond the categories of utility and productivity.[24]

There is a supernaturalism that practically blinds itself to the vision of the gratuitousness of the whole created reality and therefore never really comprehends redemption and liberation. Redemption transforms a man according to the law of the Spirit and opens to him the full horizon of God's gratuitous presence in his creation. It is a liberating presence for those who accept the law of the Spirit and live in joy, peace, and thanksgiving, because they allow the Spirit to free them from selfishness and to open their ears to the cry for liberation of the whole creation.

Directly opposed to this is an attitude that locks one's self up in one's own ego, in self-centeredness and pride and the desire to exploit others for one's own goals and self-enhancement. Thus one falls into the sin against the Spirit.

23. Charles Curran, *Christian Morality Today: The Renewal of Moral Theology* (Notre Dame, Ind.: Fides, 1966), p. 31.
24. Gutierrez, op. cit., pp. 195–96.

The words of the Lord, "Whoever slanders the Holy Spirit can never be forgiven; he is guilty of eternal sin" (Mt. 3:29 and 12:32) have caused many discussions among biblical scholars and theologians. Unfortunately, the discussions about sin against the Spirit have often distressed people of good will, especially those burdened by anxiety neuroses. Therefore we can never insist enough that whoever prays and is willing to seek gradual liberation from egotism can be absolutely sure that he has not committed a sin against the Spirit. This horrifying sin is possible only when a person, enlightened by grace and having received the testimony of faithful Christians, still refuses the risen Lord and decides firmly and finally for that egotism that produces the bitter fruit of "fornication, impurity and indecency, idolatry and sorcery, quarrels, a contentious temper, envy, fits of rage, selfish ambitions, dissensions, party intrigues, and jealousies; drinking bouts, orgies and the like" (Gal. 5:19–21). The danger of a progressive and final resistance to the Spirit begins when one who has received the gospel does not want to orient his life according to the gifts of God in gratitude, but makes himself the center of his life and uses even the law for self-justification and security.[25]

One comes to a more profound understanding of the law of the Spirit, the law of grace, as fundament of liberty and liberation, as one develops a creative spirituality and spontaneous forms of prayer which, at the same time, are expressions of openness to the Spirit and to one's neighbor, and of creative liberty in the praise of God and in the search for his will on earth. Christian spirituality opens one to the Spirit who renews both the hearts of men and the face of the earth.

A good basis for a spirituality of liberation could be the *Magnificat*. Mary's whole life synthesizes praise of God, humble service to the neighbor, and vigilance for his needs. The great theme of her life is the liberation that comes from

25. G. C. Berkouwer, *Sin* (Grand Rapids, Mich.: Wm. B. Eerdmans, 1971), p. 340 ff.

the new Israel, the Servant, who is Christ and all who follow
him, and the liberation and salvation of those who, through
the power of the Spirit, recognize their poverty and unite
with their fellow men in solidarity. The mighty, who manipulate their neighbor, their fellow man to enhance their power,
are thrown down from their arrogant heights, and the rich,
who seek only themselves in everything, are sent away
empty. A prayer life, as expressed in Mary's *Magnificat*, is
clearly situated in the tradition of the prophets and of Christ
the Prophet. What can better prepare Christians to become a
leaven of liberation?

(d) *The law of Christ*

When the apostle Paul speaks of the "law of Christ" in his
letter to the Galatians, his great theme is the liberty for which
Christ has redeemed us. "My brothers, we are no slave woman's children; our mother is a free woman. Christ set us free
to remain free men. Stand firm, then, and refuse to be tied to
the yoke of slavery again" (Gal. 4:31; 5:1). Paul also men-
tions that he had to withstand Peter "to his face" in a prophetic confrontation (Gal. 2:11–17); for even among the disciples, freedom sometimes has to find its way by accepting
and facing the conflict situation.

Paul knows well the constant battle waged between incarnate selfishness (*sarx*) and the spirit. Everyone has to
crucify in himself that old selfish man if he is to contribute to
liberation and produce the harvest of the Spirit, "love, joy,
patience, kindness, goodness, fidelity, gentleness, and self-control" (Gal. 5:22). It is in this context of a liberating love that
Paul speaks of fraternal correction: "We must not be con-
ceited, challenging one another to rivalry, envying one another. If a man should do something wrong, my brothers, on
a sudden impulse, you who are endowed with the Spirit must
set him right again very gently. Look to yourself, each one of
you: You may be tempted too. Help one another to carry

these heavy burdens, and in this way you will fulfill the law of Christ" (Gal. 5:26–6:2).

It is clear, then, that the law fulfilled in Christ, the Prophet, demands both gentleness and courage, kindness and *parrhesia* —that is, boldness and frankness. One who accepts the law of the Spirit, the law of Christ as norm of his life will always and everywhere stand against oppression, against exploitation, and against all the contaminating forces in his environment. However, he will do so humbly, without arrogance, fully aware that he too is in need of further liberation.

(e) *Christ, the Prophet, and the Liberating Truth*

The proposed synthesis of a theology of liberation is not possible without recalling the centrality of the ethical prophetism that culminates in Christ, the Prophet. When Christ proclaims the good news to the poor and opens the eyes of the blind, he is also challenging the mighty and the wealthy. He wants to open their eyes to their own malice and free them from their alienation. He calls them to a commitment to free the oppressed and to rescue the persecuted.

When Christ unmasks the pride, egotism, and hypocrisy of the Pharisees, he does so in order to give man a real chance to be free. "The truth will set you free" (Jn. 8:32). Christ never involves us in explanation of abstract truth. For instance, he never teaches about the existence of the devil, just to assert the point. The word he proclaims, and that he speaks out in his life and death in the Paschal mystery, is always a resounding call to total conversion, a summons to come home to God in total renewal of one's heart and life. It is always an invitation to commit oneself to the liberation of all men.

Christ is the Prophet who sometimes shocks his listeners by plainly denouncing falsehood and hypocrisy, while at the same time he is Peace, the Reconciler, nonviolence incarnate. Confronting him, the sinner can accept his frankness and prophetic boldness because, in Christ, judgment is never an end in itself; he is disturbing the false peace only to invite to repentance, to healing and liberation. There is no way out of blindness, alienation, and the slavery of sin without sorrow, the pain of repentance, and conversion.

What Max Scheler explained so profoundly about the interdependence of sorrow and rebirth can also be applied to the relation between conversion and liberation.[26] Each sin, if not healed by sorrow and readiness to change one's life, puts man on the road to disintegration and enslaves him in unfreedom. Only in clear confrontation with the sinful past can man find a future of liberty.

What is true for individuals applies also to social groups, nations and cultures, and especially to the Church. Only by facing boldly the dark powers behind our backs, our individual and collective sins, can we pave the way toward renewed liberty and liberation. There is no future for liberty without reshaping the dark points, the material of our past. A stark confrontation with that past can become an element of liberation through the grace of Christ who is the true Liberator, the Reconciler, and the Peace.

Protest and the courage to accept conflict can produce liberation only where there is a readiness for dialogue, forgiveness, and collaboration. Where there is strife and class hatred without forgiveness and without any perspective of reconciliation, Christ the Liberator is absent. Protest is a powerful and liberating force if inspired by the messianic peace and carried on with peace of mind, nonviolence, and commitment in solidarity with all men of good will, especially with those who are believers in Christ, the Reconciler and Messianic Peace.

Christ, nonviolence incarnate and saving protest, also gives us direction for approaching such basic problems as war and revolution. A moral theology that has discussed exclusively the limits of a "just war" but has made no effort to work out a well-founded theology of peace, liberation, and promotion of

26. Max Scheler, *On the Eternal in Man* (London: SCM, 1960) and *Vom Umsturz der Werte* (Leipzig: Bertelsmann, 1919).

justice and reconciliation, has been pure evasion and alienation, and often has been a real temptation.

The same is true today about a theology of liberation and
the question of the use of violence and of violent revolution.[27] In the light of Christ, the Prophet and liberating Truth,
it makes sense to discuss extreme situations that might justify
the use of violence, but only if we who discuss it have first
committed ourselves wholeheartedly and have gathered all
our energies in a united effort for nonviolent action. If violence or violent revolution become our passwords, then we
are fleeing Christ, who is liberation and nonviolence personi-
fied. In saying this, I am not intending to exclude all use of
force and violence in extreme cases, but what matters here is
insistence on priorities, on the proper perspectives and proportions. It is true that Christ once expelled from the temple
those who had made it "a den of robbers"; but, his whole life
bears witness to the victory of nonviolent love and action.

4. Capital Sins Against Freedom

I trust that this discussion on the dimensions of freedom
and the mission of Christians to be a liberating presence in the
world has unmasked a number of sins against freedom and
liberation:

It is a capital sin against Christ the Liberator to look at one's
freedom merely to excuse oneself after having sinned, instead
of asking the fundamental question, "Why was I so blind, so
distracted, so unbelieving? Why did I not commit myself to
that conversion and so regain my freedom and make myself a
center of freedom?"

It is a capital sin against freedom to consider one's moral
and social life as static, indulging, in a security complex and
thus rejecting the fundamental calling to progress, refusing to
accept the necessity and possibility of a lifelong conversion.

27. Bernard Häring, *A Theology of Protest* (New York: Farrar, Straus
& Giroux, 1970).

Those who preach individual conversion without committing themselves to social, cultural, economic, political, and ecclesial renewal are sinning against liberty and liberation. The same applies to those who call only for social, cultural, economic, political and ecclesial change without any commitment to personal conversion.

Passivity is a source of many sins against freedom, and it has serious consequences. An education that stresses only submission and represses spontaneity, creativity, and the spirit of courageous initiative sins greatly against freedom. We must emphasize over and over again that anyone who proposes a static vision of morality and conformism commits a serious sin of alienation from freedom. Especially is this true in today's dynamic world.

Another capital sin against liberty and liberation, and against the development of responsible and coresponsible persons, is an exaggerated paternalism or a centralism that promotes a mode of education and a way of governance that condemns the majority of persons to underdevelopment of their freedom and of their capacity for responsibility.

A disincarnate spiritualism also stands as a capital sin against liberty. Such a "spirituality" is often little more than flight from the world and refusal to take up one's own personal responsibilities in the world.

A basic sin against freedom and liberation is unreadiness to listen to prophets.

Among other great sins against freedom today is the consumer mentality, a capitalism that promotes attitudes that allow, with an all too good conscience, the abuse of things and even of persons.[28]

A mortal sin against freedom lies in any form of exploitation or seduction of persons and any unjust manipulation of public opinion. These things represent total contradiction and opposition to freedom and responsibility in the social and per-

28. John Macquarrie, *Paths in Spirituality* (New York: Harper & Row, 1972), p. 121.

sonal realms. This is the capital sin of the totalitarian states, where a kind of brainwashing is imposed on all and where there is no allowance for the organic formation of sound public opinion. In an important discourse of May 1, 1955, Pius XII denounced this sin in the secular world and sharply rebuked its occurrence within the Catholic Church. He specifically noted that it can be a sin "of the pastors as well as of the faithful." The point is that not only in totalitarian regimes but even in so-called free societies, only a few persons and powerful groups dispense the means of communications, control the mass media, and thus can and often do manipulate public opinion. This situation calls for enlightened protest and common liberating action.[29]

A common sin against freedom, whether by people in government or those in the community, is to take "the easy way out" by yielding to pressure groups. A citizen's lack of interest and nonparticipation in social, political, and cultural life is also sinful; and still more so is a pedagogy that fails to prepare young people for competence and responsibility in these fields, thereby negatively affecting the whole history of liberation.

Devastating on all levels is an ethics and pedagogy of prohibition that never offers a constructive plan but only tells what "not to do" in the great problems of individual and social life. We think, for instance, of the question of birth regulation. Where churchmen offer no more than indiscriminate and sharp condemnations of all contraceptive means, they could become partially accountable for an increasing trend toward abortion. Physicians and therapists interested in prophylactic medicine often encounter similar blocks to all reasonable tentative solutions of hard cases.

29. On the problem of manipulation, see *Concilium: The Manipulated Man* (May 1971). The whole issue bears on this argument. See also Vance Packard, *The Hidden Persuaders* (New York: McKay, 1957) and Erich Fromm, *Escape from Freedom* (New York: Holt, 1941). On manipulation in the fields of medicine and psychoanalysis, see Bernard Häring, *Medical Ethics* (Notre Dame, Ind.: Fides, 1973), pp. 58–64, 176, 204.

Finally, if we fail to reserve for ourselves time, occasions, and places for reflection and prayer, with a view toward deepening and preserving our inner peace and our awareness of our mission to the world, we sin against liberty and liberation. Whoever believes in the history of liberation set in motion by Christ has to prepare himself to be a credible witness to the peace and liberty he wants to promote.

5

Mortal and Venial Sin

Karl Rahner assesses the pastoral norms on sacramental absolution issued by the Congregation of Doctrine, June 16, 1972, as lacking awareness that there is a problem about how to determine mortal and venial sin.[1] I am convinced that pastoral norms for the celebration of the sacrament of reconciliation, and laws about individual confession and general absolution, cannot be given today without a keen awareness that there is a problem. This must be made evident in this chapter.

1. History of the Problem and the New Situation

If we compare the history of moral theology in past centuries with that of the first thousand years, we are struck by the disproportion in efforts given to determine what constitutes mortal and venial sin. The moral preaching and teaching of the first centuries realized, of course, that there was a gradation among sins. There were always warnings about those dangers that could easily turn man away from God. It

---

1. Karl Rahner, "Bussandacht und Einzelbeichte, Anmerkungen zum Römischen Erlass über des Bussakrament" in *Stimmen der Zeit* 190 (1972), pp. 363-72.

was, however, only after the sacrament of penance had taken its present form[2] that there was a real obsession in the minds of moralists and of scrupulous people to determine accurately what was mortal and what was venial sin.

The approach must be evaluated in the total context of culture and in the light of the Church's self-understanding at the time. Ecclesiology informs us that when law and control, particularly assertion of the Church's direct or indirect power over all events in the secular world, came to the foreground, when the Church simultaneously exercised her authority in the secular realm with the methods of the secular culture and uncritically carried this over into the spiritual realm, it became possible for the moralists to spend disproportionate energy on the accurate determination of what God—or rather the Church—imposed under pain of mortal sin.

Rigoristic trends brought about total confusion by indiscriminately connecting grave sin with mortal sin and all venial sins with daily sins of weakness or "less serious" sins. The situation worsened under the impact of Jansenistic rigorism, which took hold in great parts of the Roman Catholic Church. Sectors of the reformed churches were doing no better. Their brand of rigorism asserted that the greatest part of humanity is doomed to eternal condemnation and this by powerful divine decrees from the very beginning of time. Thus was created and spread a terrifying image of God.

Adhering to the teachings of the most rigoristic medieval theologians, Calvin preached that "everything is mortal because it is a rebellion against God's will that necessarily provokes his wrath."[3] Calvin emphasized that if sins are pardoned by God, it is not so much because of their venial nature but because of God's mercy. The other side of the

2. Through the Irish-Scottish monks, and adopted and regulated through the Fourth Council of the Lateran (1215) and finally through the Council of Trent.

3. "*Omne peccatum mortale est quia est adversus Dei voluntatem rebellio quae ejus iram necessario provocat.*" Calvin, *Institutio* (Bk. 2, Ch. 8, no. 59).

coin is that God is not obliged to pardon any sin; he is just; each sinner deserves the death penalty, that is, eternal damnation. For both Calvinists and Catholics, the rigoristic concept of sin produced innumerable traumas. The Pilgrim Fathers, as the South African Calvinists today, helped themselves by seeking, in their material success, signs of God's pardon and election. Catholics became scrupulous, and many were confessing the most trifling faults with meticulous care in order to ensure their salvation even while overlooking guilt of real sins.

Considering the accusation of atheism that if there were a God, he would surely be infinitely greater than the one we have manifested, we are forced to examine thoroughly our approach to the problem of mortal and venial sin. However, many other reasons besides secularism and atheism force and help us to consider the question in a new light. The outcome will not be a less serious outlook but one more faithful to revelation and more helpful to men of this day and age. At least this is our hope.

Over and above the general reasons for a new approach to sin in a secular age, there are particular reasons for re-examining the whole problem of the distinctions between mortal and venial sin. A change of emphasis and perspective is inevitable, first of all because of a deeper and renewed self-understanding of the Church. She now sees her role more as an educator toward maturity and discernment than as a controller of behavior. She goes beyond restrictive laws to proclaim the gospel with a clearly affirmative orientation. She realizes that conscience stands supreme before God, that it is hard if not impossible to judge the conscience of a man in a specific instance. The emphasis has shifted from an externally imposed order to firmness of faith and sincerity of conscience.

The comparison of cultures, sociology, and anthropology have shown that what is considered a great disorder in one culture can be, in another culture, a step forward from a markedly imperfect situation to a less imperfect one. Depth psychology and social psychology have made us more circumspect in judging others and even ourselves. Often what we believe to be fully deliberate, and therefore free, can have its roots in the many repressions of the subconscious. However, more than anything else, it is a better knowledge of the Bible and a deeper appreciation of the whole tradition that free us from a faulty approach to the question of mortal and venial sin.

2. Important Distinctions

Why do we maintain the traditional distinction between mortal and venial sin? There is a growing consensus among moralists that it is unacceptable to equate grave sin with mortal sin and venial sin with slight or nonserious sin.

Mortal sin is always grave, as death is grave. It is a refusal of God's friendship, opposition to the Covenant, and total alienation of the person from God, from himself, and from the community. It is a fundamental option against God and, explicitly or implicitly, a conscious idolatrous option for one's own egotism or idols.

Venial sin is like sickness. Not all sickness is grave, but it would be an absurdity to assert that every ailment to the point of death is in the "nonserious" or "slight" category. It would be equally absurd to claim that no venial sin can be grave.

There is an essential difference between mortal and venial sin. When compared with what we mean by "mortal sin," the concept of sin can be only analogous in the case of venial sin. Yet there are great differences among venial sins. Those sins that indicate the beginning and advance of decay, a gradual loss of zeal and increasing alienation, must be distinguished from the sins of weakness or daily sins of those persons who are sincerely on the road of conversion. For them, venial sin is like a minor detour or unwarranted hesitation along the right path. On the contrary, the person who is aware of a progressive deterioration and alienation from God has little to gain by comforting himself that his sins are probably only venial sins if there is no firm purpose to return to his previous fervor and to accept the basic law and need of continuous conversion. On the other hand, a person who has truly made his option for a life of ongoing conversion should not be unduly pained even while experiencing some serious defects. According to traditional rules, such a person can firmly trust that he has not committed mortal sins, especially if each time and soon after his fall, he has renewed his contrition and his purpose of amendment.

3. THE BIBLICAL VISION

Holy Scripture does not explicitly offer the distinctions regarding sin as outlined above; they are the result of theological and pastoral reflections. However, we have to return constantly to the Bible in order to redefine our traditional distinctions, emphases, and perspectives, and to protect ourselves against an unbiblical application of our distinctions.

There is no doubt that the Bible itself often points clearly to a graduation of sin,[4] but the *Sitz im Lieben* of it is never a distinction between mortal and venial sin in view of an obligation to confess or not to confess sins. The main context is already in the Old Testament: the urgent call to conversion, whether from a total or a partial alienation.

The call to conversion becomes particularly urgent for Israel, since she has received the Covenant and the law of the Covenant as well as many other signs of God's goodness and mercy. The sins of Israel are therefore held to be more serious than the sins of those who have not had the same chance to know God. In Israel's prophetic preaching, the gravity of sins seems to correspond to a lack of gratitude. Because God's graciousness has revealed itself to man, the greater is man's sin if, by lack of gratitude, he forgets God and refuses his will.

4. G. C. Berkouwer, *Sin* (Grand Rapids, Mich.: Wm. B. Eerdmans, 1971), pp. 285–322. A great help for catechetical presentation is Eugene Maly's *Sin—Biblical Perspectives* (Cincinnati: Pflaum, 1972).

The greatest sin is committed by that part of Israel which, despite the full manifestation of God's love in Jesus Christ, refuses the new Covenant.

If the sin of the early Israelites who rejected the law of the Covenant was greater than the sins of the Gentiles, then far graver is the sin of those who, in a lively community of faith, have come to the knowledge of Christ and have nevertheless turned away from him and his law of love. "If we willfully persist in sin after receiving the knowledge of the truth, no sacrifice for sins remains: only a terrifying expectation of judgment and fierce fire will consume God's enemies. If a man disregards the Law of Moses, he is put to death without pity on the evidence of two or three witnesses. Think how much more severe a penalty that man will deserve who has trampled under foot the Son of God, profaned the blood of the covenant by which he was consecrated, and affronted God's gracious Spirit! . . . It is a terrible thing to fall into the hands of the living God" (Heb. 10:26–31). It seems that this text applies only to the final refusal of Christ by those who had profound knowledge of Christ through faith.

In Matthew, the Lord speaks similarly about those who throughout their lives have been "a bad tree" and made mockery of the Lord's kingdom by giving only lip service while deciding against his holy law of merciful love. In the end he will tell them, "I never knew you; depart from me, you workers of iniquity!" (Mt. 7:23). The text refers to those who are guilty of *anomia*,[5] that final and total refusal of God's love, mercy, and justice, the ultimate sin of those who have met Christ, to whom he has revealed himself and who, in lying orthodoxy call him "Lord, Lord," while their whole religion is a lie that hides their obstinate refusal of God's holy will.

The sin of the Pharisees is definitely characterized as

5. I use the Greek word *anomia* because of its very specific meaning in the New Testament; it would probably not be realized if I used the English word "anomie."

anomia. "Outside you look like honest men but inside you are full of hypocrisy and iniquity *(anomia)*" (Mt. 23:28). The biblical word typifies the absolute opposition of the anti-Christ against Christ (Mt. 24:12).

It seems also that in the first letter of John (3:4) the meaning of *anomia* is the decisive rejection of God's loving will manifested in Christ and synthesized in the love of neighbor as true witness of faith. It is therefore complete alienation. But St. John insists that the true believer does not commit the sin of *anomia*. Therefore the sins of believers who continue to seek and to love Christ are of a totally different nature.[6]

The Old Testament often gives catalogues of sins that are thoroughly incompatible with the Covenant (Deut. 27:15–16; Hos. 4:24; Is. 35:15; Ezek. 18:5–18, 22:16). Similar are the lists of vices in the New Testament, indicative of those attitudes that cannot be reconciled with a sincere acceptance of the kingdom of God (Mt. 25:41–46; I Cor. 6:9–10; Gal. 5:19–21; Rom. 1:24–32, 13:13; I Pet. 4:3; II Pet. 2:12–22; Rev. 21:27, 22:15).

We must always be mindful that these catalogues were never compiled for the purpose of telling us what must be confessed to the priest as mortal sin; they were intended to be a call to total conversion. The man who is converted to Christ will launch an offensive against these vicious attitudes often typified by the Pharisees, the Gentiles, or nonbelievers. To those who have chosen Christ, these lists of sins serve the purpose of aiding discernment. They unambiguously point to what can never be done in the name of Christ or in the name of redeemed love.

Obviously, this perspective bears little resemblance to the discussions of those posttridentine moralists who sought to determine mathematically, through quantitative methods, the boundary lines between venial and mortal sin. While the

6. E. de la Potterie, "Le péché c'est l'iniquité" in *Nouvelle Revue Théologique* 70 (1956), pp. 785–97.

catalogues of this kind of sins speak strongly of the imminent danger to salvation for those who indulge in them, they do not allow that differentiation that accurately delineates the components for the venial or mortal quality of an individual act. One actually engaged in the eradication of these attitudes can take a rather optimistic stance even if, at certain moments, he is overcome by frailty.

The strongest statement on the gradation of sin is found in the first letter of John where he speaks of "deadly sin": "If a man sees his brother committing a sin which is not a deadly sin, he should pray to God for him and he will grant him life —that is, when men are not guilty of deadly sin. There is such a sin as deadly sin, and I do not suggest that he should pray about that" (I Jn. 5:16). Total refusal of God's law (*anomia*) is total alienation from God (*harmatia*); but there is also a type of sin that is only a partial alienation, which is not a deadly sin (cf. I Jn. 5:17).

John knows well that the disciples of Christ are also beset by partial alienation: "If we claim to be sinless, we are self-deceived and strangers to the truth. If we confess our sins, he is just and may be trusted to forgive our sins and cleanse us from every kind of wrong; but if we say we have committed no sin, we make him out to be a liar, and then his word has no place in us" (I Jn. 1:8–10). Nevertheless, John shows how different is the situation of the disciples of Christ in comparison with those who commit "deadly sins." "We know that no child of God is a sinner; it is the Son of God who keeps him safe, and the evil one cannot touch him" (I Jn. 5:18). St. John trusts that those who place their faith in Christ do not commit a "deadly sin." In their deepest self and option, they do not oppose the holy will of God. However, we must be ever aware that all Christians are in need of constant conversion, and that some are in particular need of the prayer and help of their fellow Christians.

The context of the first letter of St. John is quite different from the context in which the forms of the sacrament of penance have actually evolved, first in the Celtic tradition and then in the Western Church since the Fourth Council of the Lateran (1215), and especially after the Council of Trent. There are, however, common points of concern between St. John's letter and the canonical penance of the ancient Church in the case of Christians who had separated themselves from the Church. The community had to be alert to the sad situation of those who give lip service only to Christ, while refusing his law of love and mercy in the most crucial matters.

The apostolic community remains firm in the conviction that Christians can remain in friendship with Christ if they accept the call to ongoing conversion and their lofty vocation to a holy life. The true Christian does not belittle his weaknesses; he submits himself humbly and gratefully to the law of grace. "My brothers, not many of you should become teachers, for you may be certain that we who teach shall be judged with greater strictness. All of us often go wrong" (James 3:1-2). They are therefore in need of mutual help and encouragement. Christians should humbly confess their sins to one another and pray for one another (James 5:16). Disciples of Christ pray daily for the forgiveness of their sins just as they pray for their daily bread (Mt. 6:12; Lk. 11:4).

St. Paul speaks of truly serious and deplorable sins, on dangerous imperfections and deficiencies in the apostolate. Some are not building their lives on the only valid foundation, Jesus Christ, with works of "gold, silver and precious stones" but rather with "wood, hay and straw." "The day of judgment will expose their work, for that day dawns in fire, and the fire will test the worth of each man's work. If a man's building stands, he will be rewarded; if it burns, he will have to bear the loss; and yet he will escape with his life, as one might from a fire" (I Cor. 3:12-15). It seems clear that, for Paul, there can be serious faults which, however, do not deserve final condemnation. They are not in a true sense "mortal sins," yet the appeal to conversion is most urgent, a warning against the danger of falling into attitudes that could finally exclude one from the kingdom of God.

The conclusion drawn from all this is that only a moral and pastoral theology whose main purpose and perspective is conversion as response to the coming of the kingdom of God can remain faithful to the biblical message and can speak meaningfully today about distinctions of sin. The Bible does not authorize men to make judgments about whether the sins of their fellow men are venial or mortal. Nevertheless, the Christian community can judge that some people cause great harm to the community of faith by their behavior and therefore should be urged to do penance, and that those who separate themselves completely from the community of believers are severing themselves from the life of Christ.

4. FORMULATIONS OF PRECONCILIAR CATECHISMS

The various catechisms used prior to the Second Vatican Council have almost identical expressions and formulations. We commit a mortal sin if we transgress the law of God in a grave matter, with full knowledge (deliberation) and perfectly free will; we commit a venial sin if we transgress the law of God in a less important matter, or if we transgress the law of God in a grave matter but without full knowledge and/or full freedom of will.[7]

These formulations are surely not adequate for the formation of a mature conscience. They confuse the whole problem of distinctions between mortal and venial sin. The formula seems to insinuate that an accurate line can be drawn quantitatively, separating grave from unimportant or less serious matters. It does not mention that a small quantitative difference can never account for the total qualitative difference between mortal and venial sin. There is no indication of synthesis, of how the two elements that make venial sin possible—

7. See the *German Catechism,* par. 81 ff.; The *Dutch Catechism* (1910). q. 284 and 287; *Dutch Catechism* (1948), q. 381; *Baltimore Catechism* (1884), q. 56.

the object of the act and the imperfection of the act itself—are related to each other.

If the difference between mortal and venial sin arises from a merely objective distinction between more and less grave matters, without any substantial consideration of the status of man, his particular culture, and so on, such formulas invite in many ways to laxism as well as to rigorism. Those who have five talents can then, without scruple, hide four of them in the earth, so long as they have fulfilled the minimum law, while those who have received less than one talent and who, therefore, find themselves less able to cope with the line demarcating mortal from venial sin, can only fall into despair.

The catechisms' inadequate mode of discussion on the imperfection or perfection of the act fails to alert about dangers of misunderstanding. It provides a thousand motives for self-excuse. Where do we ever find perfect knowledge, perfect deliberation, perfect liberty? The least we can expect from a catechism is a more careful formulation about *proportionate* knowledge, *proportionate* deliberation and freedom—that is, the degree of knowledge and freedom that is commensurate with the penalty of mortal sin, namely, eternal damnation.

5. THEOLOGICAL REFLECTION

I remind the reader again that the focus of today's theological reflection is not the actual legislation of the Church about compulsory confession. Its goal is rather a clearer biblical vision, a better knowledge of the whole tradition, and a deeper understanding of the needs and problems of today's world. Since biblical times, the Church has repeatedly approached theological problems according to specific needs. Our obligation today is to approach it as people of our era, living in this age of secularization.

The Church of antiquity submitted certain sins to canonical penance but with no intention of declaring or categorizing them as a complete catalogue of mortal sins. In all local communities the sins of apostasy, murder, publicly known adulterous relationships, and abortion of an ensouled fetus were equally submitted to the canonical long-lasting penance. Some local churches submitted all sins of adultery to public penance, and each church could add one or another sin to the catalogue. The criterion, however, was not that of the Bible (the distinction between deadly sin [*anomia*] and daily weakness) nor the more recent criteria known to us for distinguishing between venial and mortal sins. In those times, it was the scandal that was important, the damage the sin would cause the credibility of the Church and her mission in the world.

At no time did the early Church intimate that only those sins submitted to canonical penance were mortal sins. She always proclaimed the biblical catalogues of sins opposed to the acceptance of the kingdom of God; and only those who repented of these sins with a firm resolution to overcome them could receive the Eucharist. No doubt was left that internal sins could be of such gravity as to exclude one from the kingdom of God.

When canonical penance was discontinued about the sixth century, a new form of penance emerged in the Celtic churches, in Ireland and Scotland. The old rule that absolution would be given only once in a lifetime was broken in favor of absolution whenever there was serious conversion and readiness to do penance. Second, the catalogue of sins that had to be confessed to the priest was greatly amplified. There was also an evident gradation of sins at least implied by the determination of the accurate tariff—penance—for each sin. However, these determinations from the "books of penance" that served confessors did not suggest that all the sins contained therein, and only those sins, were mortal. The penance was proportioned according to the external act only; it did not take into account the individual's degree of responsibility.

When, during the eighth and ninth centuries, the Celtic

version of the sacrament of penance was adopted over the greater part of the Continent, there was a growing concern for interiorization, a trend already quite evident in the theological renaissance at the time of Charles the Great. Abelard emerged as one of the strong voices opposing the external, quantitative measurement of guilt or wrong-doing. More and more the call for conversion of the heart was coming to the foreground in theological works on penance. However, the imposition of objectively determined penances in the sacrament of penance remained still widespread.

The vision of great theologians like Thomas Aquinas, Bonaventure, Abelard, and many others, which emphasized the fundamental option of man's heart, was in strong competition with the approach of the canonists who were more concerned for precise external control than for discernment about profound attitudes of the heart of man.

The decrees of the Council of Trent on justification and the sacrament of penance[8] correspond to the best theological endeavors and keep as main perspective conversion from alienation (first conversion from total alienation corresponds to the "first justification" and then the ongoing conversion corresponds to the "second justification"). The Council of Trent gave theology all chances for healthy development. However, under the impact of legalism and the empirical sciences, with quantification as the primary means of objectification, the moralists of the seventeenth and eighteenth centuries yielded all too often to quantitative and merely objective determination.[9]

Study of the history of moral theology yields a truly liberating result. It brings out the fact that the "tradition" of the legalistic manuals of moral theology represents a rather recent tradition and one that was never universal. Even among

8. Cf. Denzinger-Schönmetzer, Nos. 1528, 1544, 1667–93.

9. See A. M. Meier, *Das peccatum mortale ex toto genere suo—Entstehung und Interpretation des Begriffs* (Regensburg: Pustet, 1966), esp. pp. 371–82. K. H. Kleber, *De parvitate materiae in sexto: Ein Beitrag zur Geschichte der Moraltheologie* (Regensburg: Pustet, 1971).

the more conservative and casuistic moralists of the past centuries a protest was not uncommon against the all too quantitative and objectified considerations. It is only by opening our eyes to the full spectrum of earlier traditions in the whole Church that we can approach this and other crucial problems with Christian freedom.

Up to now the best of tradition has always been aware of a specific qualitative difference between mortal and venial sin, even to the point that the concept of sin cannot be used in the same sense for mortal and venial sin. In comparison to mortal sin, a venial transgression can be called "sin" in an analogous sense only; therefore, the difference between the two cannot be of a mainly quantitative character. Mortal sin deprives man of his friendship with God. It expresses and determines in man's innermost being an absolute alienation from God, in full opposition to the history of salvation and liberation. Venial sin, however, by definition in the whole of tradition, never has the power to deprive a man of God's friendship, although it can cause most serious dangers of alienation.

A quantitative approach never came to the mind of the great medieval theologians. They tried to see the problem from the viewpoint of God: It would be a perfect absurdity and even a blasphemy to assert that God takes his will and his commandments seriously only up to a certain point. Arthur Landgraf, who has made a major contribution to the investigation of the history about venial sin, asserts that after St. Bernard "perhaps no scholastic has ever dared to doubt the principle that everything that is against God's commandment is a grave sin."[10] Landgraf here interprets "grave sin" in the sense of mortal sin. Medieval theologians emphasized the word *against* God's commandment. Their understanding comes close to the *anomia* of the Bible—that is, a total refusal of the law of God. They insisted that the fully free and deliberate refusal of one commandment means, on principle, a

10. A. Landgraf, *Das Wesen der lässlichen Sünde in der scholastik Thomas von Aquin* (Bamberg-München: 1923), p. 199.

total refusal of God's will. However, insofar as they did not realize all the dimensions of man's imperfection, their own principle caused them great difficulty in explaining the possibility of venial sin. They did not fully understand the depth of man's alienation and his weakness even in conscious decisions.

Some followed Scotus by asserting that venial sin would not be transgression of a *commandment;* it could possibly be explained as neglect of a counsel. But none of the great scholastic theologians of the Middle Ages drew the conclusion that later characterized the theology of John Calvin, who taught that "every sin is mortal because it is rebellion against God's will which necessarily provokes his wrath."[11] This concept befits both Calvin's image of God and his concept of predestination in his doctrine: Since all men are sinners, all deserve eternal damnation if God so wills.

However, we do justice to Calvin only if we see his pastoral, pedagogical intention. He wants to insist that everyone should put his trust only in God's undeserved mercy and never in his own justice according to law. Further, he wants to inculcate that conversion means total adherence to God's will. Calvin's position can be understood only as reaction to those Catholic theologians who wanted to determine by inches the precise point at which God's will is to be taken seriously, and below which the transgression of God's commandment falls short of the character of serious sin.

A Catholic contemporary of Calvin, Johannes Major, taught that theft from a rich man's harvest of from one to five ears of grain was no sin; that theft of from six to ten ears was a venial sin, and theft beyond eleven ears made it a mortal sin.[12] In his rigorism, Major was not far behind Calvin. If a man deserves eternal damnation for gleaning from a rich man's field eleven ears of grain, then it seems that Cal-

11. Calvin, *Institutio Religionis Christianae,* Bk. 2, Ch. 8, no. 59.

12. J. Major, *Quartus sententiarum,* ed. Ponset Le Preux (Paris: 1509), Dist. 15, q. 19, fol. 4, 99.

vin's position is more coherent than that of Major and his friends.

A number of moralists tried to explain how the smallest quantitative difference could be the reason for the absolute qualitative difference between mortal and venial sin. Often, they used the example of Claudius Lacroix,[13] who explained that just as one additional drop of water can sink a boat, so one more drop of alcoholic beverage can make a man drunk and thus render him guilty of mortal sin.

In modern theology, it seems self-evident that the solution cannot be found in the direction of quantitative determination. Our renouncing of geometric determinations of what is mortal sin and what is not goes hand in hand with our readiness to renounce the desire to judge the conscience of our neighbor as to whether he has committed a mortal or a venial sin. An attempt to offer people quantitative determinations is opposed to the main task of moral theology, namely, to call to radical conversion.

The possibility that a transgression of God's law can be only venial sin, as in fact it is in most cases, is based on man's imperfection and on his being inserted in a sinful, alienated world that therefore allows only gradual development of his moral insight and freedom. The degrees of freedom and moral insight are so different that any effort to determine the exact dividing line between mortal and venial sin becomes a shocking form of alienation from reality, in addition to its being depersonalizing.

Our point of departure is the fact that not every act and action of man truly expresses the person in his totality. Mortal sin is a fundamental option in the sense that it happens only where a sinful human act arises from the depth of conscience, or reaches out into that depth, and thus reveals man's fully accountable misuse of the liberty that truly expresses and determines man in his total existence. Most of the relatively

13. C. Lacroix, S.J., *Theologia Moralis* (Cologne: 1729), Bk. 3, Part 1, dubium 2, no. 1101.

free acts of man do not bespeak his whole self, but they do contribute in one direction or another to a person's total self-determination. It is therefore impossible for us to declare venial sins as nonserious, since they can lead to a gradual diminution of moral freedom to a point of eventual final breakdown.[14]

Whatever provokes man's free decision under the impulse of concupiscence, his own partial alienation, or the pressure of a hostile environment can become mortal sin only if it penetrates to the inner depths of the free person. Given sufficient knowledge and commensurate freedom, man realizes that it is a matter of decision that sets a final orientation to his life; thus he declares himself against friendship with God, against solidarity in good in favor of solidarity in evil. The decisive element of a mortal sin, therefore, is the fact that the act arises from one's deepest being, from one's own malice of heart, and with such knowledge and liberty as to represent really self-determination against God. If I say "the act" I do not think of an isolated act, but on the whole development that constitutes the decision for total alienation.

This approach in no way negates the objective importance of the act and decision, but the object or gravity of the matter assumes meaning only in proportion to the actual development of a person's knowledge and freedom in such a way that it can evoke that deep self-determination we have described. We can generally say that attitudes that, in the Gospel, are characterized by total opposition to the kingdom of God represent a radical call to conversion for every Christian; if one who has reached a normal level of development refuses to oppose them in his heart, he cannot abide in the state of grace.

With respect to the object of the act, we can say that grave sins normally constitute such great disorders, cause such damage or scandal to the community that no one who is psychologically and morally developed can ignore that by his act

14. Cf. Chapter 4 on liberty and liberation.

he willfully separates himself from God. Those who have attained a certain degree of moral insight and freedom can also realize that there are internal decisions, acts of the heart, that are in opposition to man's ultimate goal. However, there is no possibility whatsoever of giving a general quantitative and exact determination of where mortal sin begins.

For those who are not satisfied with or are uneasy about these criteria, I should like to say that it is much more important, and with the help of God's grace much easier, to turn humbly to God and commit oneself to true conversion of heart and life than to rack one's brains about the venial or mortal liability for one's past actions. The more a person is ready to search for God's will in all things and to continue patiently on his road to conversion, the greater can be his certainty that he is in the state of grace.

This solution to the crucial problem of mortal and venial sin is a pastoral one: it is an urgent appeal to accept the law of grace, which means to receive God's gifts, one's own particular talents, and the present opportunities as expressions of God's will, and never to yield to the temptation to make mathematical calculations about the upper and lower limits of God's will in order to remain "safe" from sin.

What I especially want to communicate is an intuition of the unfathomable condescension of the holy God, whose commandment of love demands absolute seriousness but who, at the same time, knows our fragility and limitedness. He alone knows accurately the grace he has given us and the amount of freedom at our disposal at any time. This alone should be enough to move all men of good will to serve God with joy and total commitment.

I also want to emphasize again that this approach to the thorny problem of mortal and venial sin is possible only because, according to the scope of tradition and biblical teaching, the focus of our moral theology is not so much confession as conversion. If the problem has become insoluble, it is principally because of an undue emphasis on the role of the confessor as judge. In no way do I intend to deny the validity and the present canonical obligation of the decree of the Council of Trent that one has to confess all mortal sins of which one is conscious before receiving communion. However, I am convinced that a moral theology that serves life will also provide a better perspective for understanding the sacrament of reconciliation.[15]

The value of the sacrament of reconciliation for individual and social salvation does not depend at all on this obsession with determining what has to be confessed under law as mortal sin. The sacrament should be celebrated and received gratefully as proclamation of the messianic peace and as personal and communal commitment to the kingdom of justice, peace, and liberation. A confessor is, above all, a brother among brethren who, assisted by the law of grace, proclaims the necessity of continuous conversion and renewal. Thus he turns the penitent's attention to Christ, the Healer, who bestows his healing and reconciling action on whoever gratefully accepts his gifts.

The present discipline obliges Catholics to confess before receiving communion all mortal sins of which they are conscious. Since I know that many good people are troubled by this regulation, mainly because the official doctrine is not always well understood, may I remind the reader about some traditional rules of prudence?

It must not be forgotten that Church law imposes no obligation of this kind whenever a person has good reasons to doubt whether the sin he has committed was subjectively a mortal sin. After an act of sorrow and purpose of amendment, he can receive communion with trust and joy. He will con-

15. It is some twenty years since I proposed this vision in the first German edition of my book *The Law of Christ* (1954), and to my own surprise, it immediately found consensus among the majority of theologians who have expressed their opinion on this subject. See Bernard Häring, *The Law of Christ* I (Westminster: Newman Press, 1959), pp. 352–64; bibliography, pp. 382–84; and P. Schoonenberg in *Mysterium Salutis* II, pp. 854–61; bibliography, pp. 939–41.

fess at the convenient time the sin that he considers a serious one but hopefully not a mortal sin. This rule should be followed especially by persons who tend to be scrupulous or anguished. So long as a person, who generally displays good will in the following of Christ, sincerely doubts having committed mortal sin, the presumption is always in his favor, provided he can sincerely say before God that he is seeking his friendship and trying to discern his will.

Another useful traditional rule is that a person who generally displays good will but is particularly weak in some respect and falls from time to time, but who renews his contrition and the firm purpose of continuing his fight against sin soon after his failing, can and should hope that he has not committed a mortal sin.

These traditional rules promote neither laxity nor anxiety. However, the point should be made that such traditional rules are of no help to salvation for persons who wish only to avoid mortal sin, without truly seeking God's will, and therefore do not care to avoid serious venial sins. It would be as if someone said that he does not want to die but is neither willing to avoid sickness nor to seek treatment for ailments, no matter how grave they may be.

I think the approach that I have proposed also makes it easier to understand and appreciate one of the main norms given by the Congregation of Doctrine, June 16, 1972, namely that a Christian should not restrict his reception of the sacrament of penance to mortal sins.

The communitarian celebrations of penance and conversion should be more positively evaluated for what they are. They stand for more than a good preparation for individual confession; they can be very effective and visible signs of ongoing conversion and renewal, of the commitment of persons and communities to reconciliation on all levels. With Karl Rahner I would express myself in favor of their sacramental quality. Although the decrees of the Council of Trent that all mortal sins should be confessed remain binding for the time being, our discussion of the serious and dangerous character and social impact of so many venial sins provides enough evidence in support of the importance of communal celebrations of conversion and reconciliation.

6. CAN CHILDREN COMMIT MORTAL SINS?

If our reflections on mortal and venial sins have any foundation, then it is evident that we cannot speak of mortal sins in children. Canon 906 of the Canon Law seems to suggest that children, from the moment they come to the age of discernment (*ad annos discretionis*), can commit mortal sins because they come under the obligation to confess annually in the sense of Canon 901. As we have seen, this canon binds in strict obligation only those who are conscious of having committed mortal sin.

No civil government, even of the most authoritarian and totalitarian type, would intimate that children of seven, eight, or ten years of age can commit a crime deserving of the death penalty. What image of God do we present if we speak of mortal sin for immature adolescents and even children? Mortal sin carries the same gravity as a crime that would be deserving, in the eyes of the infinitely merciful God, of eternal abandonment and total alienation. The discernment required for the reception of first communion is one thing, but totally different is that discernment that conditions the possibility of subjectively committing a sin great enough to deserve eternal condemnation.

I am not saying that the sins of children and adolescents are not serious or dangerous so long as they cannot commit mortal sin carries the same gravity as a crime that would be de- of gradual development, conversion, and liberation, then it is obvious that the years of development of a young person are most decisive. Therefore, the Church has to give great attention to the moral development of children and adolescents; the religious and moral education should begin as early as possible and be in accord with their psychological and cultural situation. Children should be gradually introduced to the meaning of sin, contrition, and a humble confession of their sins. As soon as is possible, they have to understand that life is a continual conversion and purification; if a person refuses such a vision of life, he exposes himself to great danger. A dynamic moral and religious pedagogy combined with communal celebrations of conversion and reconciliation, and individual confession, will help a young person to realize ever better the importance of a firm orientation. Youth have to be brought to an understanding that each moral decision has consequences and carries a positive or negative weight in the dynamics of community interaction.

7. Does the Final Decision Happen Before or After Death?

A new consideration of the dreadful character of mortal sin relative to the pain of eternal rejection has led respectable theologians to a new theory suggestive not only of a distinction between grave and mortal sin but also of one between mortal sins that may happen repeatedly during one's lifetime and the mortality of the final decision that alone would deserve eternal condemnation.[16] I do appreciate the theory of these theologians as an effort to react against a moral theology that seriously misrepresented God as if he could be more cruel in condemning people to an eternal jail than any human tribunal. I think we should be extremely careful in stating what deserves eternal condemnation. Eternal damnation can be part of God's glorious creation only if no one is eternally condemned who does not fully realize he has deserved it.

16. Karl Rahner, *On the Theology of Death* (New York: Herder and Herder, 1961). R. Troisfontaines, *Je ne meurs pas* (Paris: 1960), pp. 109–61. L. Boros, *The Mystery of Death* (New York: Herder and Herder, 1965). P. Schoonenberg, "Grade der Sünde" in *Mysterium Salutis* II, pp. 858–59.

However, this theory can mislead Christians if they do not understand the context and intention; I wish, therefore, to voice a critical warning. First, the theory is not proposed as an assurance and no one should be tempted to escape from life's decisions by a false trust that he will be able to undo everything at the moment of death or immediately after. Second, this theory is not sufficiently grounded. The conviction of the whole Christian tradition is that the decision for eternal salvation must be made during life in the body, during that time of favor granted man by God. The hour before one's death is surely not to be undervalued; that is why Christians pray perseveringly for a peaceful hour of death. If, in accord with the traditional doctrine, we say that the hour of death is decisive for our eternal salvation, we mean the last decision made freely while we live in the body.

Those who accept the new theory as probable must be sensitive to the intention of those who propose it. They should be aware that the ultimate decision, which they surmise would happen immediately after the separation of soul from the body, is prepared positively or negatively by the sum of all the decisions of one's lifetime in the body.

According to Catholic doctrine, God graciously gives final purification after death to those who, during their lifetime, did not attain perfection but had chosen God as their ultimate goal. It is in this sense that tradition speaks of *purgatory*, and it is a most consoling truth. Rightly understood, it gives added incentive to use well this time of decision in our earthly life.

I believe that in addition to infants who die before the use of reason, there are also many adolescents and adults who have never during their earthly life attained that degree of knowledge and freedom that makes possible and thinkable an eternal rejection of God. We trust, then, that God in his kindness will bring them to wholeness. We do not need to know how.

8. MORTAL SIN EX TOTO GENERE SUO?

A certain Catholic tradition that thought that the borderline between mortal and venial sin could be quantitatively determined has also insisted that there are some areas of sin in which there is never possible an excuse from mortal sin on behalf of a "smallness of matter"; with other words, in certain areas— for instance in questions of orthodoxy in thought and word, magic practices, directly intended transgressions of the sixth commandment—every degree of disorder was considered as mortal sin. This was meant by the traditional expression "mortal sin *ex toto genere suo*," that is in all its dimensions. In these fields the traditionalists renounced to a quantitative measurement which, however, was stressed regarding all other kinds of transgression of God's commandment, even where respect for man's dignity, mercy, and justice are directly involved.

As we have seen, any quantitative measurement of sin is so unrealistic and so depersonalizing as to be absolutely unacceptable, especially in today's milieu. With Marxist collectivism seeking to guarantee equality by the imposition of the same quantitative measurements on all, and by total submission to the party line, we are all the more allergic to any mathematical approach to moral and religious questions. But the suggestion of mortal sin *ex toto genere suo* in some areas is hardly better since the choice of these areas and the kind of criterion it offers is quite arbitrary and sometimes includes what is obviously trivial.

A distorted image of God and a real temptation against faith would result from a teaching according to which in most areas a small quantitative difference regarding the amount of disorder would justify the absolutely qualitative difference between hell and purgatory, that is between mortal and venial sin. Fortunately, contemporary moral theology is attempting a radical revision also of traditional categories which led to the idea that in some fields of morality every fault would be a mortal sin while in all the other areas mortal sin would begin only at a certain point of disorder which was determined with a quantitative measurement (this was called mortal sin *ex genere suo*). Strange enough in some fields which today's world considers as rather important every fault could be considered as merely venial sin (*veniale ex genere suo*).

Sensible men have always realized that these categories and distinctions could serve only as a rule of thumb. They could be understood as a form of strong warning: Danger! Attention! But they become senseless if they are to be used as criteria by a judge who wants to draw for his average penitent a borderline of quantitative nature between mortal and venial sin. In other words, it makes sense to warn people that in the most crucial moral fields there is extreme danger to eternal salvation and to the common good. But the warning cannot be intended as tolerance to take God's will seriously only to a certain point in other matters.

A prophetic warning, moreover, cannot be given in abstract or general terms that pay no attention to the diversity of cultures, situations, and personal development. One can speak and warn prophetically only if he has knowledge of actual life situations and is able to read the signs of the time. A moral theology that wants to stimulate conversion and shake the superficial conscience has no place for abstract classifications or precise measurements of personal sins. In this regard, it is also interesting to discover from scholarly studies that the traditional concept of *peccatum mortale ex toto genere* has often changed its meaning throughout the centuries, and that it does not fall within common tradition.[17]

Traditional moralists of the past centuries held that all sins committed directly against God, including all sins against faith and hope, are always mortal sins; they never allowed for triviality of matter. Of itself, the assertion expresses an important concern for the urgency of growing in the knowledge of

17. A. M. Meier, op. cit., pp. 221–43, 336–45.

God, in the love of God, and in adoration. However, in trying to apply such an abstract principle, moralists often betrayed a great lack of knowledge of the condition of man. For instance, in the treatises dealing with mortal sins of superstition and magic, they included such marginal things as expressions of atavism, which we more realistically attribute only to human weakness and to ridiculous attitudes of the environment. Can we truly say that the average man realizes fully that these things are irreconcilable with God's friendship?

9. Is Everything Against the Sixth Commandment Mortal Sin?

The faithful of the past centuries were particularly troubled by the specific doctrine of many moralists that all sins against the sixth commandment are *ex toto genere suo* mortal sins. The meaning and motives behind such an assertion were quite varied. One of the principal reasons was the sanctity of human life. For St. Thomas Aquinas and many moralists of the past centuries, the sperm of man was "something divine because the sperm is potentially a human person."[18] According to St. Thomas Aquinas, each sin of lechery, that is, against the sixth commandment, is similar to murder because "it is an attack on man's potential life because it is a disorder about the act of human procreation."[19] On the pastoral level, the assertion that all sins against the sixth commandment are mortal sins was intended to be a pedagogical warning that whenever man, with full advertence and free decision, selfishly seeks sexual pleasure, he makes himself liable to all the disorders that perforce follow so long as he keeps such deliberate intentions.

The very careful study of Kleber, *De parvitate materiae in sexto*,[20] gives sufficient evidence that the doctrine of moralists alleging everything in the sixth commandment to be mortal

18. Aquinas, *De malo*, q. 15, art. 11.

19. Ibid., q. 2, art. 10.

20. H. Kleber, *De parvitate materiae in sexto: Ein Beitrag zur Geschichte der Moraltheologie* (Regensburg: Pustet, 1971).

sin if committed with full deliberation and freedom, took on different meanings and often met with opposition from theologians in good ecclesial standing. Therefore, it is impossible to claim common conviction or an official doctrine of the Church on this point.

What matters in this field is the authority of good reasoning and good argument. I think it is quite evident that today's moralists concur more and more on the thesis that the sixth commandment is subject to exactly the same norms as the other commandments. How can one who follows a biblical perspective easily accept the levity of matter with respect to charity, justice, and peace while asserting that in matters of chastity everything is mortal sin?

The arguments on the problem can go in two different directions and come to almost identical conclusions.

(1) In one direction we can start with the thesis that in all moral areas, every perfectly deliberate and free act that expresses a profound decision of conscience against God's will cannot become venial solely through the relative smallness of the external object of the act against God's will. We apply the same principle to the sixth commandment and try to give reasonable meaning to the traditional doctrine of those numerous moralists who held that in sins against the sixth commandment, committed with direct and full intention and freedom, there is no smallness of matter. In that case, we do not allow exception in any other commandment. We follow the best tradition among those Catholic moral theologians who warned that nobody can stubbornly transgress the sixth commandment to a certain point without danger of mortal sin, stressing with them that we speak only of acts having fully the character of a free and deliberate decision. However, we reject the position of moralists of the past centuries who so easily assumed, with regard to all sins against the sixth commandment, even to the matter of *delectatio morosa* (sexual fantasies that cause inordinate pleasure), that the average Christian would at all times have at his disposal such perfect

knowledge and liberty that his transgression would be commensurate with eternal damnation.

In the other direction, we can go along with traditional expressions only to the extent of firmly emphasizing that in no commandment is there any possibility of determining the point at which God would not take his commandment seriously and where a person could deliberately transgress it with the assurance that there would be no danger of mortal sin. Allegiance to God's will is integral, whole. At the same time, we insist that nobody who generally seeks God's will should be anguished after minor sins of weakness, since God knows man's weakness and frailty. Today's moral theology is more deeply aware of the sin in the world and of the extent of alienation in man's environment. Since man comes only gradually to a normal level of liberty, we should not even dream of the average man having such keen consciousness, such perfect power of deliberation and freedom that in daily affairs, including matters of chastity, he would always have at his disposal such full freedom to express himself in all situations with a final decision or fundamental option.

(2) On the practical level, we come to the same results if we take as point of departure the rule of prudence that a man of average development does not fully realize and actualize his freedom in the decisions that involve matters that to him seem less important. This applies to the sixth commandment as well as to all the others. The conclusion is that if a man has not explicitly acted with malice and bad purpose, although he has partially yielded to temptation but not in important matters or by offending God through relatively serious external acts, the Christian of good will can always abide in the hope that he has not committed mortal sin.[21]

I do not intend to minimize the importance of chastity or of self-control in the full development of freedom and liberation. However, with respect to sexual education, the rigorism that compels people repeatedly to reconsider their past, about

21. Bernard Häring, *The Law of Christ* III, pp. 291–98.

whether or not they have committed a mortal sin, heightens the very danger it tries to combat. It can be a source of obsessions and lead to diminution of freedom.

Moral theology must always maintain a pedagogical orientation. A constructive approach that leads to serenity and peace of mind is much more conducive to chastity than a rigorism excessively inclined to judge each sin of weakness against chastity as a mortal sin. The heart of a person's whole moral life is unselfish love, openness to the other, respect for the other and for himself. Such an orientation is likely to lead to continued development and conversion, and enables the believer gradually to overcome his difficulties in chastity as well as in other fields.

6

Can Human Laws Be Imposed Under Pain of Mortal Sin?

Most of the sins of which the average preconciliar Christian accused himself in devotional confession were sins against the laws of the Church rather than against the law of God proclaimed in the Gospel and inscribed in man's innermost being. At this juncture of Church history, in view of her renewed self-understanding, we cannot avoid another thorny problem: Can the Church impose under pain of mortal sin something that is not demanded by man's own nature and by the Gospel? This question needs to be considered in the broader context of whether man-made laws can oblige conscience and under what conditions.

1. AUTHORITY IN THE SERVICE OF CONSCIENCE

The exercise of human authority, whether by parents, a secular society, or particularly by the Church, becomes a moral factor only when the directives, orders, laws, and precepts through a clear manifestation of the values involved appeal to the moral conscience. The transgression of a human precept or man-made law can be morally culpable only when the intrinsic malice of the transgression is recognized, at least by implication. For example, children feel obliged in conscience to obey their parents because by seeing and experiencing the love and moral seriousness of their parents, they are deeply convinced that what their parents ask is good.

The just laws of the state protect the freedom of all, the right of all persons to the development of freedom, and the citizens' basic rights and values against arbitrariness and abuses of freedom by individuals and groups unwilling to respect the fundamental rights of others. However, we are faced with the sad reality that all too often the exercise of human authority does not promote moral health but rather becomes a deterrent to moral development. Such is the case when the primary motive in the exercise of authority is a demonstration of power, control for control's sake, the manifestation of a domineering attitude, and the exploitation of individuals or groups. The situation becomes even worse when those who abuse authority and impose unjust laws attempt to manipulate the conscience of their subjects by hypocritical and superficial appeals to moral motives, even to the point of bringing into play a threat of sanctions for the life to come.

2. ALIENATION OF CONSCIENCE THROUGH MISUSE OF AUTHORITY

Depth psychology has provided evidence that many neuroses, especially in the form of guilt complexes, have their origin in infancy through the child's anguish about being punished, but most of all through the fear of losing the love of his parents. This false guilt complex is one of the main obstacles hindering man from coming to authentic faith and trust in a God who is Love.

In an era characterized by atheism and serious crises of faith for so many believers, the Church has to ponder these findings of modern psychology. She must examine particularly her right to impose laws under grave sanctions. If she threatens so easily with loss of God's friendship and eternal damnation, does she not become responsible for guilt neuroses? Is she not misleading man by a false concept of "justice according to law"? Does not the disproportion of her emphasis on petty man-made laws imposed under pain of mortal sin, compared with the less serious treatment of the great commandment of love, cause many forms of compensatory scrupulosity, individual or collective, on the one hand, or alienation on the other hand? If a person already suffering under a neurotic guilt complex, caused by childhood threats of loss of love, later meets unreasonable threats by Church authorities that he will be punished with eternal fire if he transgresses their laws, then the obstacle to faith becomes almost insurmountable.

Contemporary theology can no longer escape the question of whether the Church has the right and the competence to impose her man-made laws—that is, positive laws—under threat of eternal condemnation. By positive or man-made law I mean something that is not a part of the absolute demands of human nature (natural law) or of revelation.

3. The Lessons of History

History teaches us harsh lessons about the gravity of this problem. As early as the first centuries, two Roman bishops threatened all the churches of the Orient with the breaking of the eucharistic unity if they refused to accept the Easter date that the Roman Church had chosen. However, in those cases the Roman bishops yielded to the prophetic voices of holy men who had come from Asia: Polycarp and Irenaeus. To be sure, the Roman bishops did not use the phrase "under pain of mortal sin," but to threaten the loss of what is most essential for the Church, namely the eucharistic unity, the greatest gift of God to the Church, as a means of imposing a man-made law about something like an Easter date, is a shocking historical instance of the same frame of mind.

The Constantinian era brought in its wake innumerable temptations to use religious sanctions and threats of eternal punishment to enforce laws that did not serve the Gospel or the development of the human person, laws that were directed more to the temporal order and especially served the alliance of throne and altar. All too frequently the sword of excommunication and threat of eternal condemnation were used in the Church's struggle for direct power over the temporal order.

The greatest culprits were probably the moralists of the past centuries who so often decided upon the sanction of mortal sin for Church laws that really had little particular relevance for anyone. They often seduced Church authorities to make public such sanctions. Under pain of mortal sin, many things came to be imposed: absolutely regular assistance at Mass on all Sundays and prescribed feast days, abstinence from meat on Fridays and during the Lenten season, the fasts during Lent and other specified times of the year, Eucharistic fasts from midnight, to the point that some moralists dared say that the person who had taken one drop of water, or had not spit out a tear rolling down his cheek, would commit a mortal sin if he received communion. The exclusive use of the Latin language in liturgy and in Church teachings was made mandatory under innumerable threats of mortal sin, and liturgical celebrations themselves were surrounded by hundreds of rubrics and prohibitions that liturgists, rubricists, and moralists considered binding under pain of mortal sin. The consequence was that fear of committing sin became infinitely greater than the joy of celebration.

Some moralists also contrived the doctrine that a short hour of the breviary obliged under pain of mortal sin; if this were neglected through human weakness, in full awareness, one would deserve eternal condemnation. Finally, the Church added to the Gospel and natural law a number of invalidating laws that moralists always considered as binding under pain of mortal sin. The best known is legislation about marriage, whereby many marriages that naturally, by consent and intention, were valid according to the order of creation, were declared invalid if the Church's form of celebration and other conditions were not observed.

Karl Rahner expresses well the reaction of modern man when he asks, "Who today would dare to attribute so easily to ecclesiastical precepts, even down to trifles, the character of an obligation under pain of mortal sin?"[1]

A number of moralists even asserted that the Church, through a positive law, can impose under pain of mortal sin what by natural law comes only under the heading of venial sin![2] The surprising fact is, however, that none of these theologians has ever questioned himself as to the kind of image of the Church, and even of God himself, such an opinion reflected. A better knowledge of man, a more serious vision of the power of evil's investment in man's heart and in the world around him, and a greater concern for credibility have now made such *naïveté* impossible.

4. Toward a Solution

We are far from having resolved all problems. There remain a number of open questions. However, I dare to offer some points of departure:

(a) No man-made law can hold power to oblige conscience if it is arbitrary. Human authority and human law can oblige man in conscience or appeal to conscience only if they can show the necessity of the law or precept, or at least its usefulness for the common good and for the development of responsibility and the freedom of the person.

(b) The positive laws of the Church must be thoroughly

1. Karl Rahner, "Bussandacht und Einzelbeichte" in *Stimmen der Zeit* 190 (1972), pp. 363–72.

2. "Salmaticenses," *Corsus Theologicus*, Tract. 13. *De vitiis et peccatis*, disp. 10, dub. 5 (Paris: 1877), Vol. 7, tit. 374, no. 185.

subordinated to her mission to educate toward conversion. Her main task is to proclaim the Gospel and, through the Gospel of the kingdom of God, preach thorough conversion. All her positive laws must be in the service of the "law of grace" and "law of faith." The laws of the Church that go beyond the Gospel and beyond what is inscribed in the hearts and minds of men must come in response to the signs of the times, and therefore cannot bind beyond the historical context making them necessary.

(c) The positive law of the Church must never unduly generalize or be imposed on people of vastly different cultures and social conditions if it is not truly something that is necessary for the best of all these people. Legislation of the Church that does not take into account the diversity of cultures and situations cannot truly bind conscience. A sad example was the constitution *Veterum Sapientiae*, which Pope John signed under the pressure of his environment and for which, he openly confessed, he made many acts of sorrow. It sought to impose, under obligation of conscience, the use of the Latin language in the liturgy and in the teaching of philosophy and theology throughout the world. Not only did it disregard the diversity of cultures and the tremendous danger of separating religion from life, but it also revealed complete ignorance of what modern philosophy and the sociology of language have made very clear, namely, that language is always related to a cultural context.

(d) If parents are very kind and just, their children will have a spontaneous trust that what their parents ask is good. But if parents start punishing or mistreating their children and threatening them about unimportant matters, children will not have the same intuition into and trust in the goodness of what the parents demand. In a paternalistic age, if church authority was trustworthy and had good officials, people had a confidence similar to that of children toward their parents; they felt that what the church required was good.

It is psychologically impossible for today's critical adult to accept a grave obligation to obey a man-made law if those who promulgate it cannot offer adequate reasons and motives for its binding force. Not only can obligation under pain of sin—and especially under pain of mortal sin—arise only from the importance and urgency of the law itself and never from the mere will of the legislator, but also this urgency and relevance must be made clear not just by sanction but by persuasion, by insight. If modern man is faced first by sanctions and threats of eternal damnation, he will never feel a true appeal to his conscience. Exaggerated sanctions and threats of punishment can never awaken the holy fear of God; they awaken only a pseudoconscience that leads to all kinds of neuroses and that can be one of the greatest obstacles to true faith in a God who is love.

(e) In my opinion, the Church should never impose any man-made law under threat of mortal sin, which means threat of eternal condemnation. The reason is that I cannot imagine any positive law that is neither part of the gospel nor of the natural law written in man's heart therefore not discovered through shared experience and reflection, and yet could be so important as to be proportionate to the threat of eternal punishment.

We are dealing here with an interesting aspect of the sociology of religion: religion in its interdependence with the environment. We have to remember how governments and even moralists of the past so easily justified capital punishment, "pain of death"; but cultural progress, new insights, and greater attention to the gospel have led most states to abolish the death penalty. Moralists cannot so easily justify it now. Yet the consequence of mortal sin in Church doctrine is infinitely greater than capital punishment; it means eternal hell, eternal alienation from God, endless imprisonment within the solidarity of corruption.

The Church has to be faithful to the teaching of Christ, who often warned people about the danger of eternal damnation; but the actual problem is how we can speak convincingly of this truth to modern men who are aware of the enormous exaggerations of moralists and priests who have multiplied the threats of mortal sins with regard to trifles and to laws of the Church about minutiae.

If the Church speaks of the danger of eternal damnation, she should stay within the catalogue of dispositions that, according to Scripture, exclude from the kingdom of God. Such attitudes reveal rejection of the call to conversion and an unwillingness to combat those alienating tendencies that are in contradiction to the kingdom of God.

It is my conviction that a positive law that cannot be presented as an exigency of the gospel or of man's own nature can never have such urgency as to justify capital punishment in the grave sense of eternal rejection in hell. I am not speaking of contempt or rebellion against authority that is instituted by God. Such a revolt would mean rebelling against an essential part of the Gospel and an attitude clearly opposed to the solidarity of salvation preached by Christ. But if protest against officials and authorities is provoked by intolerable exaggerations, by misuse of authority, and above all, by the imposition of trifles under pain of mortal sin, the sin of those who provoke such a rebellion may be infinitely greater than of those who suffer psychologically from oppressive tactics.

(f) The sanction *sub gravi* added to a positive law can simply mean that it is an important matter and that those who would not put it into practice are incurring the danger of offending God gravely, in the sense of a grave venial sin, not necessarily in the sense of a mortal sin. No doubt, the Church can make us alert to the fact that refusal to observe very important positive laws can constitute a grave danger for the development of our Christian freedom and our insertion into the community of salvation. But according to the traditional manuals, the sanction *sub gravi* truly meant threatening with hell; consequently, promulgation of some laws *sub gravi* intended to assert: "Transgression of such a law will be punished by eternal condemnation." Insinuations of this type should be absolutely excluded wherever it cannot be proved clearly that the precept or law is an absolute exigency of the Gospel or of man's being created in the image and likeness of God. If a warning need be given, let it be in respect before God, in full knowledge that God does not take men's orders. It must always be evident that the warning arises from God's own Gospel.

5. Some Classical Examples

The approach to this problem is best clarified by some examples. I will take three that are important in themselves.

(a) *Penitential works*

Penance, in its deepest sense, is an absolute exigency of the gospel. It involves the urgency of radical conversion for whoever has alienated himself from God, and the urgency of continuous conversion for those who are in the state of grace but in need of further purification, as we all are. It also includes the readiness to atone for one's own sins and to fight persistently all forms of personal and group egotism. Understood in this way, penance is surely obligatory in the most serious sense.

A totally different question is how certain external penitential works prescribed by the Church can oblige under pain of mortal sin. In the first part of the constitution *Poenitemini* of Paul VI (1966)[3] he emphasizes and describes penance in a way that practically coincides with the conversion demanded by the gospel. The Pope has the whole tradition of the Church behind him when, in this matter, he teaches that "all the faithful are obliged by God's own law to do penance."[4]

3. Paul VI, *Poenitemini* (February 17, 1966), *Acta Apostolicae Sedis* 58 (1966), pp. 177–98.
4. Ibid., p. 183.

In the second part, the constitution specifies, with great moderation, a few common celebrations of penance and a few penitential works. It insists that Lent should have its penitential character and that some days—all the Fridays of the year and the first day of Lent—should be considered by the faithful as days of penance. However, it is left up to the episcopal conferences to specify in what sense these days should be days of penance and thus become an essential call for charity and for penance insofar as it fosters fraternal love and justice. About the celebrations and penitential works it is then said, "the essential observance of them obliges gravely."[5]

The Church of the Word Incarnate has to find concrete, tangible forms, certain times and ways to call Christians regularly to conversion and reflection on real penance and conversion. The words of the constitution on the grave obligation of substantial observance can be understood as a serious warning that those who are totally unwilling to accept this regular invitation of the Church to do penance, especially that penance necessary for the growth of fraternal love and justice, expose themselves to the great danger of neglecting altogether the call of the Gospel to penance. The initial words of the constitution are *"Poenitemini et credite evangelio"* (Mk. 1:15). The Latin word *poenitemini* is not a very fortunate translation of the Greek word *metanoeite*, which refers to metanoia, that conversion of heart and mind, that newness of life that is the fruit of living faith and the very response to the Gospel that calls us to a renewal of life.

While a meticulous observance of small penitential rituals and works could be an immense evasion or flight, indeed an alienation, the real meaning of the apostolic constitution is an incarnate preaching of the Church in which the penitential rituals and works become only symbols, although real symbols, of the call to total conversion. Those who understand

5. Ibid.

and accept this meaning will also give attention to the catechetical and pedagogical effort of the Church.

(b) *The priestly prayer and prayers*

By God's calling and grace, the Church is a "house of
prayer" (cf. Luke 19:46). To call and to educate all the
faithful, and particularly priests and religious, to a profound
life of prayer constitutes one of the most fundamental tasks of
the Church. Therefore, the Church of the Word Incarnate
also has the right and obligation to guarantee in a concrete
way the continuity of prayer and the necessary means for all
to learn how to pray better, to remain faithful, and to give
each other mutual support. It is quite in accordance with the
mission and main concern of the Church to set up particular
laws for priests and religious on how to promote their charism
in solidarity, to learn how to pray and to foster the spirit of
prayer in the whole Church. Therefore, the Church's law
relative to the divine office is not mere advice with no obligation; it is a law that truly binds conscience.

With respect to our particular problem about whether the
Church can impose mere positive laws, I would say that there
is an aspect that is only a positive law, but there is another that
truly belongs to the substance of the law of grace. To learn
to pray, to help one another in the life of prayer so as to transform our life into praise of God, "adoration in spirit and
truth," is a matter of life and death for the whole Church, for
each of the faithful and, in a very special way, for the priests
and religious, because God has bestowed on them a particular charism for prayer, to the betterment of the whole
Church.

Meticulous casuistry about the quantity of divine office,
which would oblige under pain of mortal sin, can only obscure the evangelical calling to a life of prayer and give rise
either to minimalism or to a lack of flexibility in the Church
with respect to appropriate forms of prayer. On the one

hand, it would be senseless to determine the point at which God takes seriously our calling to prayerful vigilance for his coming. It would be equally against the Gospel and would obscure the image of God to assert that the Church wants to condemn to hell a priest who, instead of reciting the breviary, is seeking, alone or with others, a way of prayer and meditation that helps him toward greater spiritual growth. It must be evident that the Church seeks primarily to be helpful.

(c) *Regular attendance at Mass*

The most delicate example relates to the obligation to assist regularly at Mass on all Sundays and prescribed feast days. Here again, it is above all a problem of pedagogy. One cannot doubt the centrality of the Eucharist for the whole life of the Church and of the faithful. However, the Church would fail greatly if she were to present the Eucharist primarily as a law. The Eucharist is grace, a great gift of God, and therefore Eucharistic education must help Christians to understand this character.

It is an absolute absurdity to present the Eucharist, under threat of hell, to children of seven or even ten years as something they must assist at under pain of mortal sin. Obligation becomes a dynamic force and a strong appeal to the conscience of a Christian only if the Church grants him the experience of this great mystery of faith, this effective visible sign of unity and solidarity, in a feast of joyous acceptance of the Covenant of Christ and of his word, as a source of renewal of life and of continuous conversion. Only through the knowledge of these intrinsic values can the law then become a binding force for conscience. For instance, a priest would be guilty of "sacred lies" if he wanted to impose regular assistance at Mass in his parish when the Mass is celebrated hastily, without joy, without communication of the gladdening news, without a minimum of authentic experience that it is a visible celebration of unity and solidarity for the people of God.

The emphasis on obligation under pain of mortal sin has often been an evasion and an alienation for officials of the Church. This is the case when they have neglected a genuine Eucharistic education and a sincere effort to give to the Eucharistic celebration all its vitality and visibility. Whoever wants to determine accurately, for each individual Christian and for all parts of the universal Church, the gravity of the obligation to assist at Mass regularly, without taking into account the great lack of evangelization in some parts of the Church and the various degrees of imperfection in the presentation and celebration of the Eucharist, misunderstands the nature of conscience.

The regular rhythm of participation in the Eucharistic life is important for the community as well as for the individual person. Therefore, it cannot be denied that the Church rightly prescribes regular assistance at Mass each Sunday and feast day unless a proportionate reason excuses the Christian. But since the absolute regularity is by no means a divine law, it seems out of proportion to threaten eternal damnation each time someone exceptionally neglects Mass. This disproportion is particularly shocking if the celebration of the Eucharist is not at all attractive.

The Church also prescribes, and justly, a regular homily during Mass, but it is generally understood that, on several occasions during the year, the priest may abstain from giving the homily even if he is able to give a well-prepared one. The Church in today's world would obtain better results in her eucharistic pedagogy if she would similarly leave some margin of free decision to each person with respect to the Sunday Mass.

I consider it possible and reasonable to speak of grave obligation in the matter of attendance at Sunday Mass, but not in the sense of mortal sin. The eternal rejection by God seems to be out of proportion to the occasional neglect when it is not a case of obstinate bad will or contempt, but only an expression of human weakness or superficiality.[6]

Let us recall again, as we conclude these reflections, the key idea to this book: the phenomenon of secularization, the critical sense of the man of today, and particularly his difficulty in believing in God who is Love, after so many disillusions and jolting experiences. All this imposes on the Church a duty to rethink profoundly her pedagogy and legislation where it jeopardizes the true image of God.

6. Cf. Georg Troxler, *Das Kirchengebot der Sonntagsoflicht als moral-theologisches Problem in Geschichte und Gegenwert* (Freiburg/Schweiz: 1971). According to Troxler, St. Antonin of Florence (who died in 1459) was the first to assert that the absolute regularity to assist each Sunday Mass obliges under pain of mortal sin. However, it may be that Antonin understood *sub gravi* as I should like to understand it, namely as a warning about grave danger. One of the leading theologians of the Council of Trent, Melchior Cano, distinguished still sharply *sub gravi* and "under pain of mortal sin," for instance, when he asserted that a person who has committed a mortal sin and receives holy communion after an act of sorrow, while postponing confession by negligence, does sin very gravely (*valde graviter*), but does not commit a mortal sin (cf. I. Tubaldo in *Nuova Alleanza*, October 10, 1972, p. 397 ff.). Troxler asserts that before the Code of Canon Law (1917), Canon 1248, there was never such a law given for the universal Church. And it was never stated that regular assistance at Mass obliges under pain of mortal sin.

Conclusion

The present book on sin and salvation in a secular world is possible in this form only because its main orientation is not toward sacramental confession. It seems to me that one of the consequences is that the Church, while keeping the sacrament of penance in high esteem, has to envisage her role as educator for conversion in a deeper, broader, and more demanding sense. Her whole life, liturgy, preaching, catechesis, and ecclesiastical law have to give evidence to the true nature and centrality of conversion along with the renewal of the community and of structures, so that she can truly become a visible and effective sign of union with God and unity for mankind. The good news of the kingdom of God will always be central to a discourse on sin. The doctrine on original sin should never be abstract, but thoroughly integrated into the call to solidarity in salvation. Everything must be linked to the testimony of liberation.

Nevertheless, I should also like to draw some conclusions with respect to the crisis of the sacrament of penance. It requires as profound a revision as the theological treatise on sin. The whole Church, the hierarchy, theologians, and the laity, through dialogue and prayer, need to seek more appropriate expressions in this new era. In full consciousness of the difficulties, I venture to propose some suggestions for reflection and criticism.

1. I propose another name: "the sacrament of reconciliation" or perhaps "the sacrament of peace and reconciliation." This would be in keeping with an older tradition of the Roman Church and would draw attention to the presence of Christ, the Conciliator, and to his gift of reconciliation and peace which, by the very acceptance of the gift, calls the Christian to be messenger and promoter of peace and reconciliation on all levels. The word "penance" does not fittingly communicate the wealth of this sacrament to modern man, especially in view of the later developments of tradition which, through stereotyped penances, have thoroughly obscured the deeper significance of penance as conversion, and of the true meaning of prayer as well ("for penance, three 'Hail Marys'").

2. I would revive, but in a new form, the canonical penance of the first centuries, being careful, however, to give close attention to the causes of its earlier decay and still more to the new life situation today.

It must be remembered, however, that the canonical penance never fully embodied the sacramental grace and call to conversion. There were always various other forms of combating those attitudes that exclude from the kingdom of God, together with a deeper understanding of the whole of Christian life as ongoing conversion. The canonical penance was imposed only for well-defined public and greatly scandalous sins. What the posttridentine theology had to say about the role of the priest as "judge" should be strictly reserved for such cases. Even there, the merely analogous meaning of "judgment" must never be forgotten.

3. I propose a radical renunciation of all efforts to determine accurately what, objectively and subjectively, is a mortal sin. A warning could then be given more effectively that there are attitudes that exclude from the kingdom of God if one

does not try to eradicate them. The unrealistic determination of the dividing line between mortal and venial sin has caused anguish and scrupulosity and has often resulted in evasion; thus it has blocked the liberation of which the Church is called to be a sacrament.

Energies would be marshaled for the education of the faithful to confess their sins in the sacrament and in life, especially where it is a matter of sins that greatly endanger salvation or at least block a full breakthrough to the liberty of the children of God. The consciousness of encounter with Christ, the Reconciler and Healer, would be the predominant experience. Penitents would then consider the grace of reconciliation and messianic peace with that gratitude that makes them messengers and servants of this peace on all levels of life. A less triumphalistic Church, thoroughly aware of her own shortcomings and partial alienations, would more effectively educate the individual member to a healthy awareness of the need for his own conversion and humble confession in the context of a commitment to reform and liberation in saving solidarity.

4. The communal celebrations of reconciliation and of ongoing conversion (revision of life) should be more highly evaluated. This would facilitate an understanding of the social character of sin, of alienation, conversion, and reconciliation. The communal celebration of penance and revision of life are more than a preparation for individual confession. If their own value were fully recognized by the Church, the individual confession would also more effectively regain its social character.

5. It is equally necessary to re-evaluate fraternal correction. Inserted solely by grace into the community of salvation, each Christian is, by the very grace of reconciliation, committed to promote the sanctity of the Church and help the neighbor who is in trouble (Mt. 18:15–22; Gal. 6:1–2; James 5:9–16). Fraternal encouragement and correction, offered in a spirit of gentleness (Gal. 6:1), followed by humble

avowal of one's sin and by the prayer of the good person (James 5:16) gives particular assurance of the presence of Christ, the Reconciler, because there two or three are truly gathered in his name (Mt. 18:20). This dimension should be emphasized also in the individual confession to the priest.

6. Last but not least: the central role of the Eucharist as being celebrated always "for the forgiveness of sins," for reconciliation and peace, should be made more obvious.

Through Christ's gracious presence, not only the Eucharistic celebration itself but also the whole preparation for this great sacrament of faith, the homily and particularly the penitential rites become a calling to conversion, a calling to combat alienation in the solidarity of grace, and a mission for the liberation and salvation of the whole world.

The invitation to eat the bread of life and to drink from the cup of salvation is the most gracious challenge to live in a new spirit, to continue the fight against all those attitudes in one's own heart and in the environment that militate against the kingdom of God.

Freed from a frustrating self-interrogation as to whether they have committed a mortal sin, but always alert to the need for further conversion, Christians of good heart will see the gate of communion widely open, and their acceptance of the invitation will be an ever-renewed commitment to progressive liberation from darkness and alienation, a life that promotes the solidarity of salvation in Christ.